M000080912

WILDERNESS
WANDERINGS

Finding Contentment in the
Desert Times of Life

Stacy Reaoch

For Ben—my late-night editor, my biggest fan,
my best friend. Thanks for believing in me and loving me
through the wilderness journey of life.

– Stacy Reaoch

CruciformPress

CruciformPress.com | info@CruciformPress.com

"Our lives often mirror the Israelites' journey into and through the wilderness years: hardship, uncertainty, and doubt. And yet, the same God who provided and cared for them cares for us today. Stacy extracts for us the truths regarding God's constant character, character that he displayed to the wandering Israelites and that can sustain us even now."

Christine Hoover, author of *Searching for Spring* and *Messy Beautiful Friendship*

"Stacy Reaoch has thought long and hard about the Israelites and their wilderness journeys. In this devotional book, she peers into the doubts, fears, discontentment, and disobedience of their hearts with insight and discernment. And then she accurately and incisively demonstrates how these very realities reside in our own hearts. She focuses on the truth of God's character, God's promises, and God's ways shown throughout the wilderness wanderings, encouraging all of us to trust, fear, hope in, rest in, and obey our Redeemer and Savior. Stacy writes with clarity and creativity, using appropriate illustrations and applications. Each entry has a suggested prayer and several questions for self-examination. We highly recommend this book for careful, prayerful reflection."

Bruce and Jodi Ware, The Southern Baptist Theological Seminary

"In the midst of my own journey through the wilderness, I found myself encouraged and challenged by the biblical, insightful, and practical wisdom woven throughout Wilderness Wanderings. There is much to glean from the Israelites' time in the wilderness and Stacy does a wonderful job applying its biblical truths to our own lives."

Sarah Walton, co-author of *Hope When It Hurts: Biblical Reflections to Help You Grasp God's Purpose in Your Suffering*

"There's a reason to remember the places God's people have been and the many, many (many) times He has carried them through. We all find ourselves wandering at times. Wandering through the desert of disappointment, the desert of fear, the desert of pain. . . we need the reminder that the God who was with Moses is with us, every step of the way. Consider this delightful devotional your must-have guide for any season of wandering."

Erin Davis, author, blogger, and wilderness wanderer

"*Wilderness Wanderings* is a feast of truth for tired, busy women. Stacy points us to the Israelites' wilderness journey to draw a compelling parallel to our lives as twenty-first century women, offering us true hope in gospel grace. I wish every woman would pick up this book — but especially young women — and taste the joy, peace, and contentment that come from resting in Christ."

Jaquelle Crowe, author of *This Changes Everything: How the Gospel Transforms the Teen Years*

"Adulthood is so much harder than we expected in ado-lescence. The hills are steep, the path is not evenly paved, and the twists and turns are often treacherous. But the joys! The wilderness joys of trusting our heavenly Father, and releasing our grasp on earthly comforts, are deeper and sweeter than we could have dreamed. Stacy Reaoch is a gifted guide for real joy in hard places. She loves God, is full of his word, has walked this way herself, and is ready to take you through the stresses, strains, pains, and pleasures of desert life on the path to the Promised Land. The exodus from fear and discontent isn't easy, but oh is it worth it."

David Mathis, executive editor, desiringGod.org; pastor, Cities Church, Minneapolis/St. Paul; author, *Habits of Grace: Enjoying Jesus through the Spiritual Disciplines*

"In our struggle to find contentment where God has us, we can often feel completely alone, as if no one else has ever experienced our struggle. But Scripture tells a different story, for there we see that there is nothing we face that is not common to us all. The struggle of the Israelites to find contentment in the wilderness has a message for all of us, and Stacy helpfully offers us that message. I pray this book serves you not only to rest in God's abundant care for you, but also to know that his word still speaks even all these centuries later."

Courtney Reissig, author, *Glory in the Ordinary* and *The Accidental Feminist*

"*Wilderness Wanderings* is insightful and engaging. Pick it up as a companion to your reading of the Exodus and you will find yourself exhorted, convicted, and most of all encouraged about the great God who ultimately sent his Son to free his people from slavery to sin."

Keri Folmar, author, *The Good Portion: The Doctrine of Scripture for Every Woman* and *Joy!*, *Faith*, and *Grace* Bible studies for women

"*Wilderness Wanderings* is a tonic for the soul. Reaoch takes us through the experiences of Israel in the wilderness and deftly applies the text to our lives today. The book is biblically faithful, spiritually challenging, and encouraging. A wonderful resource for both personal reading and for group discussion."

Tom and Diane Schreiner, The Southern Baptist Theological Seminary

"Every single one of us is met with seasons of life where difficulty seemingly lingers without end. In Wilderness Wanderings: Finding Contentment in the Desert Times of Life, Stacy Reaoch seeks to help readers by faithfully taking them through the Exodus story, pointing them to Christ, and then providing them with practical guidance from the Word of God. I encourage you to pick up Stacy's book and learn the faithfulness and greatness of our God from a fellow pilgrim. In doing so, you'll be blessed by her biblically faithful exposition, her gospel-centered focus, and her practical guidance from a life lived before the face of our beloved Lord Jesus."

Dave Jenkins, Executive Director, Servants of Grace Ministries; Executive Editor, *Theology for Life Magazine*; Co-Host, The Equipping You in Grace Podcast

"Faithfulness to Scripture marks the pages of Stacy's book, as she helpfully unfolds the wilderness journey of the Israelites and applies the timeless truths of God's Word to us. Through her writing we behold our powerful, trustworthy, and wise God, the God of biblical history and the God who walks closely with us in our wilderness wanderings, right now."

Kristen Wetherell, co-author, *Hope When It Hurts: Biblical Reflections to Help You Grasp God's Purpose in Your Suffering*

"Anyone who has lived the Christian life for a season knows that following Christ inevitably means walking into suffering, trials, and discouragement. Wilderness Wanderings is a guidebook through these barren and difficult paths, and a drink of cool water for the weary traveler. Using the biblical narrative of Israel's years in the wilderness, Stacy Reaoch lifts our eyes from our dusty feet and points us to the Lord's grace and mercy in even the most trying circumstances. Arranged into a series of twenty five devotionals, this book is sure to bear fruit in the lives of readers for a long time to come."

Megan Hill, author, *Praying Together: The Priority and Privilege of Prayer in Our Homes, Communities, and Churches*; editorial board member, Christianity Today

"As Stacy leads us through the wilderness with the Israelites, keenly unveiling God's deeper purposes in their seeming aim-lessness, she also patiently testifies by her own life that it is the sovereign hand of a loving God that directs each wandering step.

She shows us that God's providence always conspires to give his children more of Christ—and it is in the desert that we learn the sweetness of the living water found only in him."

Abigail Dodds, blogger, author

"*Wilderness Wanderings* follows Israel's years in the desert before entering the Promised Land. In studying this portion of biblical history, you'll see yourself and God's faithfulness in your own desert wanderings. Like Israel, we are quick to forget all God has done in our lives. Stacy's Word-centered devotional will remind you afresh of God's unending grace and faithfulness and, above all, his provision of life in Christ."

Christina Fox, speaker; writer; author, *A Heart Set Free* and *Closer Than a Sister*

"In *Wilderness Wanderings*, Stacy Reaoch puts on her tour-guide hat and walks us through one of the most significant sections of Scripture. On page after page, Reaoch applies ancient truths to contemporary life in a style that will inspire reflection and devotion. Read and be stirred to trust the God who can part waters."

Matt Smethurst, managing editor, The Gospel Coalition

Table of Contents

Cruciform Press

Books of about 100 pages
Clear, inspiring, gospel-centered

CruciformPress.com

We like to keep it simple. So we publish short, clear, useful, inexpensive books for Christians and other curious people. Books that make sense and are easy to read, even as they tackle serious subjects.

We do this because the good news of Jesus Christ—the gospel—is the only thing that actually explains why this world is so wonderful and so awful all at the same time. Even better, the gospel applies to every single area of life, and offers real answers that aren't available from any other source.

These are books you can afford, enjoy, finish easily, benefit from, and remember. Check us out and see. Then join us as part of a publishing revolution that's good news for the gospel, the church, and the world.

Wilderness Wanderings: Finding Contentment in the Desert Times of Life

Print / PDF ISBN: 978-1-941114-52-0   **Mobipocket ISBN:** 978-1-941114-53-7
ePub ISBN: 978-1-941114-54-4

Published by Cruciform Press, Minneapolis, Minnesota. Copyright © 2017 by Stacy Reaoch. Unless otherwise indicated, all Scripture quotations are taken from: *The Holy Bible: English Standard Version*, Copyright © 2001 by Crossway Bibles, a division of Good News Publishers. Used by permission. All rights reserved.

Scripture quotations marked NIV are taken from THE HOLY BIBLE, NEW INTERNATIONAL VERSION®, NIV® Copyright © 1973, 1978, 1984, 2011 by Biblica, Inc.® Used by permission. All rights reserved worldwide.

Italics or bold text within Scripture quotations indicates emphasis added.

FOREWORD

Are you a control freak like me? From my calendar to my kitchen, from my money to my make-up, I like to create a plan and control it to completion. No wandering off course for me! How could God be pleased with that? I've got too much work to do! I'm just too busy to waste my time meandering through a day.

So when I find myself in a dry spell where all my self-important busy-ness disintegrates, where normal life gets strangled in the wilderness of a new job or the complexities of a new relationship or the desert of an unexpected loss, it's then that confusion and guilt find their way straight to my heart. And it's then that I need help—the kind of help that Stacy Reaoch beautifully offers us in this treasure you are holding in your hands.

Tracing the "Wilderness Wanderings" of the children of Israel on their way to the Promised Land, Stacy skillfully helps us see ourselves within those wanderings, showing us how much like Moses and the Israelites we really are. And then she offers us the hope of a powerful, loving, and sovereign God for our inevitable wilderness experiences.

This book is ideal for busy women who have limited time to be in the Word, but desire to study a chronological section of Scripture and see how it applies to their lives. It could be used individually, in a small group Bible study, or in one-on-one mentoring. The simple but concise thought questions that follow each devotional help guide her readers into a meaningful response to God's Word.

Winsomely relating her own experiences as a woman, a wife, and a mother, Stacy identifies with our needs as we each walk our own pathway toward the eternal Promised Land. She reminds us that with God, there is no unnoticed suffering, especially on that seemingly pointless pathway marked with injustice. She encourages us to loosen our grip on the circumstances and people we so often want to control as we walk toward Heaven.

Stacy also carefully warns us about the dangers of disobedience--not only for us, but also for those closest to us. She opens up one of my favorite biblical themes: generational blessings. She shows us God's desire for complete, heartfelt obedience. What kind of legacy do we want to leave? As you read through this book, you will be reminded that your own wilderness wanderings have a purpose, and that your responses to your present desert experience have eternal consequences.

Settle in with this gem of a book. Read it with both an open Bible and an open heart. Let it be your manna for a month or so. Say with Jeremiah, "Your words were found, and I ate them, and your words became to me a joy and the delight of my heart" (Jeremiah 15:16). Let the God of Moses and Joshua guide you through your own wilderness wanderings, giving you "drink from the river of his delights" (Psalm 36:8).

And when our days in this worldly wilderness are finally finished and we have reached the Promised Land, let's look for each other and praise our kind King together for the wonder of being included in those who sing around his Throne, "Happy are you, O Israel! Who is like you, a people saved by the Lord, the shield of your help, and the sword of your triumph" (Deuteronomy 33:29). I can't wait!

Jani Ortlund
Author; Vice President, Renewal Ministries
Franklin, Tennessee

INTRODUCTION

This past fall, my husband and I had the privilege of attending a retreat for ministry couples in upstate New York. On a clear, sunny day we had some free time and decided to take our first hike in the Adirondack Mountains. The path we wanted to follow was supposed to lead to a beautiful peak where you could see for a hundred miles. As we got ready to go, we felt excited for our new adventure. The owners of the bed-and-breakfast we were staying at warned us that it was a fairly difficult four-hour hike, but we felt up for the challenge and were eager to head out.

So off we went, armed with only a granola bar and a bottle of water. And as for hiking gear, we had none. Just sweatshirts, shorts, and tennis shoes for each of us. We were blissfully unaware of the intensity of the climb and how ill-prepared we were. As we began our hike things seemed easy enough, but the path quickly became more difficult, with slippery leaves covering the trail and steep rocks to climb. I soon realized that running shoes are not made for mountain climbing.

Our hike was marked with spray-painted red markings, or flares, on the trees. Normally you follow the same color flare to your destination—different-colored flares change the course and often the difficulty. After following the red flares on the trees, suddenly we only saw blue flares. What happened to the red? With no other hikers in view for well over an hour, we decided to follow the blue (which then turned to orange). I began to imagine our friends at the retreat calling out a search party for us as my husband and I tried to figure out which way to go.

Life can often seem like a maze. Like my husband and me on our hike, we enter adulthood with high hopes and big dreams, blissfully unaware of the challenges set before us. We don't anticipate the steep, rocky trails that will come our way through job loss or sick children or a strained marriage. We struggle to know the right path to take and can get easily frustrated along the way. At times we persevere in climbing a steep hill and then are rewarded with a glorious mountaintop view—but we can't stay on the mountaintop forever, and soon are winding back down the path, with twists and turns in every bend. We think we know the best or easiest path to take, but God often chooses a path less known, marked with unwanted difficulties that cause us to lean on him.

The wilderness journey of the Israelites on their way to the Promised Land parallels our lives in multiple ways. God's promise of an abundant land flowing with milk and honey propelled them forward, but they were met with constant struggles and discouragements along the path. From fear of enemy attacks to hungry bellies to the daunting 40-year trek, their faith in God was severely tested. And they often failed through their complaining spirits and idolatrous hearts. Discontentment was a constant companion. But our God, who is rich in mercy, gave them grace upon grace. He guided their path through a pillar of cloud by day and fire by night. And he gave them a faithful leader, Moses, to guide them along the way. A leader who demonstrated consistent love and forgiveness to a difficult and whiny people. A leader who points us to the greatest Leader who sacrificed his life for the sake of sinful man.

Throughout this devotional, you'll likely see reflections of yourself through either the Israelites or Moses or both. Our sinful hearts are not much different than the Israelites' were. And the battle for contentment rears its ugly head often in this life on earth. But I also trust you'll see the hope God offers us during our own wilderness periods. In the dark times of life where we're left wondering which way to go, God is with us. He hears our prayers and sees our suffering. He guides us by illuminating the truths of his Word and sending the comfort of his Spirit. And through the deliverance of the Israelites, he reminds us that he is faithful to keep his promises.

After many twists and turns, and moments of silent panic in my mind, my husband and I finally made it to the top of the mountain and were rewarded with a glorious landscape view of lakes, trees, and mountaintops. Despite our own wrong turns along the way, God protected us and guided us in our climb. And he even provided an easier way down via a long, windy road that had been closed for the winter. That hike tested our faith in God in multiple ways and caused us to rely on his guidance and strength to finish the course.

Nothing is wasted in God's timeline. I'm sure the Israelites had many moments when they questioned the purpose of God taking them on such a difficult and lengthy trip. Yet God is using the dark and difficult times of life to draw us to himself and showcase his own glory. Just as God miraculously parted the Red Sea to show Pharaoh and all the Egyptians that he is the Lord, God will use the trials of our life to remind us of his strength, power, and sustaining grace. Contentment isn't found in having everything turn out just how we would like, but in trusting a faithful God to give us just what we need. It's the wilderness times in life that shape and mold who we become. It's the wilderness times in life that will lead us to glory.

1: GOD HEARS US

Exodus 2:23–25

Life is full of both hills and valleys. And when we're in the valley, it can often feel dark and lonely. We wonder if anyone sees our sorrow. Does anyone notice our sadness? Does anyone care? There is something in human nature that longs to be noticed, cared about, loved. This is one reason social media has become such a phenomenon. Anyone can post their terrible day or their epic accomplishment to a world of virtual viewers who can then provide encouraging words within seconds. It can be a quick fix to lift our spirits, at least for a little while.

The Israelites were no different. They too wanted their misery to be seen and heard and noticed. They had been held captive in Egypt for centuries, working as slaves under the harsh oppression of Pharaoh. Although they had been blessed by the Lord in that they increased and multiplied greatly, on the heels of the blessing was a great sorrow: severe oppression and persecution.

As the Israelites became more numerous, the Egyptians began to fear that they would eventually mount an uprising. So they "ruthlessly made the people of Israel work as slaves and made their lives bitter with hard service, in mortar and brick, and in all kinds of work in the field. In all their work they ruthlessly made them work as slaves" (Exodus 1:13-14). Pharaoh even ordered all the male infants to be killed. It's hard to imagine the oppression the Hebrews must have felt. To be buried under loads of heavy physical labor, and on top of that, to fear that your new baby boy might be killed.

The Israelites' pain and suffering made them turn to the only One who was able to change their awful circumstances. They groaned and cried aloud to the Lord for help. And the sovereign, almighty God of the universe heard their cry. He was not immune to their enslavement and daily drudgery. He did not leave them to figure out their situation on their own. But he saw them and remembered the covenant he had made with Abraham, Isaac, and Jacob (Exodus 2:24): "The whole land of Canaan, where you now reside as a foreigner, I will give as an everlasting possession to you and your descendants after you; and I will be their God" (Genesis 17:8, NIV).

This prayer of the Israelites was the beginning of the exodus of God's people to the Promised Land. God would use their prayer as a means to start the journey from oppression to freedom.

When you are in despair, where do you turn? Whom do you cry out to? For me, it's all too easy to reach for the phone, the computer, the fridge, or my husband. Like the Israelites, we want our sorrows to be noticed and cared about, but for our rescue we often look to the things or people of this world. A piece of triple-chocolate cake can lift my spirits for a few short minutes, but that comfort is gone as soon as I'm left with a stray few crumbs and a dish to wash. Talking to a friend on the phone can bring encouragement and comfort as well, but if our conversation isn't grounded in the truth of God's Word, there is little hope to stand on.

The Lord wants us to cry out to him. He delights to hear our voice and the needs we have. He longs to be the first one we turn to when we are low in the valley. And even though he sees us and already knows our needs before we ask, he nonetheless calls us to pray to him (Matthew 6: 6-8). Our prayers for help highlight God's power and strength as the only thing that can truly rescue us.

If you are in the pit of despair right now, take heart, that your suffering does not go unnoticed. God sees you. He cares for you. And he longs for you to cry out to him for help. Whatever suffering we are experiencing is part of his greater plan to give us more of himself. It's the wilderness times of life that will lead us to the Promised Land.

Lord, help us in the midst of our suffering to lift our eyes upward. Forgive us for the times we look to the things of this world to ease our sorrow. May we find comfort knowing that you see us and hear our prayers.

Reflection Questions
1. Where do you look for help during times of suffering?
2. How has the story of the Israelites reminded you of God's care for you?

2: CAN GOD REALLY USE ME?

Exodus 3:1–12, 4:10–13

I married young. Just months after graduating from college, I wed my high school sweetheart, my best friend. We loaded the U-Haul with all our worldly possessions— basically our wedding gifts and some hand-me-down furniture from my in-laws—and moved 12 hours away from our families. It was an exciting time, for sure. But I was also apprehensive, nervous.

Having given my life to Christ during my freshman year of college, I was still a new Christian. My husband, on the other hand, had grown up in a strong Christian family and now felt called to full-time ministry. We were in stage one of the ministry training God had planned for us. Ben was to begin a pastoral apprenticeship at a large church, and together we would be working with the college students. So I was, in effect, still a pastor's wife in training. I felt *very* ill-equipped for the role. I still knew next to nothing about most of the Bible, I was trying to figure out what it meant to be a godly wife, and I was just beginning my study of the domestic arts (my failed dinner attempts had landed us at McDonald's on more than one occasion). How could I be a godly example for these college girls when I was still learning the basics myself? It seemed that God could have found much better "pastor's wife material" than me at my husband's elite Christian college.

Fears plagued me as I considered my new role. What if I were to end up meeting with a young woman and had no idea how to answer her questions? So many of these young people were attending Bible schools and probably knew far more about Scripture than I did. What did I have to offer? I felt I had so much to learn before God could really use me in the lives of these young ladies. But he had called me to this time and place, and now here I was, desperately trying to find the book of Jonah before someone realized I had no clue.

Moses felt that ill-equipped, and worse. More than once.

At the start of the book of Exodus he is called to a task much greater than himself. From a burning bush, God speaks to Moses and lays on him an enormous responsibility. He is to bring the children of Israel out of Egypt—more than 2 million of them. They had been oppressed by Pharaoh as slaves for many years, and it was time for their liberation. But Moses doesn't respond with a lot of enthusiasm. Instead, he questions God's call on his life for this task, "Who am I that I should go to Pharaoh and bring the children of Israel out of Egypt?" (Exodus 3:11).

God simply responds that he will be with Moses, and

after he has delivered the people from the Egyptians, Moses will serve God on that very mountain (Exodus 3:12).

Even with God's promises to be with him, to deliver the people, and to provide through plundering the Egyptians, Moses still doubts. He keeps thinking of excuses as to why he is really not the best choice for the job. "But behold, they will not believe me or listen to my voice, for they will say, 'The Lord did not appear to you'" (Exodus 4:1).

God answers his request by equipping Moses with miracles to perform in front of the Israelites as proof—a staff that becomes a serpent, a cloak that heals a leprous hand, water from the Nile that will turn to blood.

But still Moses resists, doubting his ability as a public speaker. "Oh, my Lord, I am not eloquent, either in the past or since you have spoken to your servant, but I am slow of speech and of tongue" (Exodus 4:10).

By this time, the Lord simply rebukes Moses and tells him to go, affirming that he is the maker of the mouth and tongue, and will give Moses the words to say (Exodus 4:11-12). Despite God's graciousness and patience with this insecurity, Moses resists one final time and begs the Lord to send someone else (Exodus 4:13-14). God's anger is kindled, but he nevertheless responds to Moses' request: God will send Aaron out to speak to the people on Moses' behalf.

It seems preposterous, arguing with God over something he has clearly called us to do. But I wonder how often we do the same thing? We refuse to say yes to an assignment from the Lord. Either by complaining, or simply refusing to do it, we take our stand. We think we know our capabilities and to what extent we can serve, but God often wants to stretch us beyond what we think is possible. Maybe you're given a new assignment at work that seems overwhelming and beyond your abilities. Maybe you just took a pregnancy test and realized you're expecting again, when your first baby isn't yet walking. Or maybe you're asked to lead a Bible study, when you feel you're ill-equipped in knowledge of the Word.

Whatever the calling may be, God wants us to remember the same thing he told Moses. He will be with us. If he has clearly called us to the task, he will see that we carry it through. He will give us the grace and the tools needed to accomplish the assignment he has given. Maybe not perfectly—in fact, probably not—but all he asks is our service, leaving the outcome to him.

Lord Jesus, thank you for the reminder that you will be with us and equip us to do whatever you've called us to. Give us the grace to not spurn our calling, but joyfully receive it and move forward in faith.

Reflection Questions

1. How have you argued with God over something he has clearly called you to do?
2. In what area of your life do you need to trust God's promise to be with you? How might he be calling you to act in a new and stretching way?

3: BLINDED FROM GOD'S PROMISES

Exodus 5:1–9, 6:1–9

Our 3-year-old son is notorious for making sweet but empty promises. When caught in the act of playing with his older brother's special and reserved Legos, he tells me with an earnest voice, "I'm sorry, Mommy. I promise *never* to do that again." My husband and I look at each other with knowing glances. As much as we'd like to believe him, we know these are probably empty words and that very likely, in just a short while, we'll find him once again digging into the same box—and once again offering another empty promise to *always* obey and *never* play with his older brother's Legos.

I wonder if the Israelites sometimes felt like God's promises were just empty words—such as his promise to relieve them from the misery of slavery.

Moses and Aaron had met with the people of Israel and told them of God's plans for deliverance and rest for them (Exodus 4:29-31). They went to Pharaoh and requested that he let the Israelites make a three-day journey into the wilderness to hold a feast for the Lord (Exodus 5:1).

Pharaoh interpreted this request as a sneaky way for the Israelites to take time off and be lazy. So he punished them: in his hardness of heart, Pharaoh made the Israelites' work more difficult by forcing them to make bricks without the straw that had previously been provided to them.

"You are idle, you are idle; that is why you say, 'Let us go and sacrifice to the Lord.' Go now and work. No straw will be given you, but you must still deliver the same number of bricks" (Exodus 5:17-18). The Israelites were more than discouraged and took out their frustration on Moses and Aaron, saying they had made the Israelites "stink in the sight of Pharaoh and his servants, and have put a sword in their hand to kill us" (Exodus 5:21). Even Moses doubted why God had sent him, since Pharaoh had only done evil to the Israelites.

But in Exodus 6 the Lord reminds Moses of his promises. He reminds him of his covenant with Abraham, Isaac, and Jacob to give them the land of Canaan. God reminds them that he hears the groaning of the Israelites. He has not forgotten them and will make good on his promises, if only they will believe. Through the promises of deliverance from slavery, God will redeem them.

Through the famous words, "I will take you to be my people, and I will be your God" (Exodus 6:7), God promises them a relationship. He promises ultimate rest through the land promised to Abraham, Isaac, and Jacob — spiritual rest and salvation despite their sins and failures. But when Moses speaks these hope-filled promises to the Israelites, they don't listen to him, "because of their broken spirit and harsh slavery" (Exodus 6:9).

Despite being offered such precious promises, the Israelites remained numb. The intense working conditions they faced under Pharaoh had robbed them of their joy and hope for the future. The promises of God must have seemed as unrealistic as finding a pot of gold at the end of a rainbow.

Difficult circumstances in life can tend to harden us. How often have you doubted a promise of God because your present situation deemed it unrealistic? Your marriage is struggling and instead of trusting God's promises to heal and transform, you assume it's beyond repair and are ready to throw in the towel. The overbearing boss at work has been making your life miserable and instead of praying for him and asking God for patience and forbearance in your own life (Colossians 3:12-13), you chalk it up to an inborn difference in personality types that has no hope of changing. Maybe your bills keep piling up and money is tight. Instead of trusting God to provide for all your needs (Philippians 4:19), you begin to fret and compare with others, allowing your heart to become jaded and envious.

Our natural, human bent is toward unbelief. We're prone to be discouraged and to allow our life circumstances to control our attitudes and actions. But the supernatural grace of God offers us something so much better. As we learn to trust in the power of his Holy Spirit, we can have faith-filled hope that allows us to bank on the promises of God's Word. Ask the Lord to keep your heart soft throughout all the twists and turns of life. Don't let a hardened heart blind you from the beauty of God's truth.

> *Father God, help us not to become hardened and without hope amidst the trials of life. When pressures surround us, help us cling to the promises of your Word. Give us faith to believe the beauty of your promises.*

Reflection Questions

1. How did the Israelites' difficult circumstances in life blind them from God's promises?
2. What situation in your own life is tempting you to ignore the promises of God? What truth do you need to believe today?

4: GOD WILL MAKE HIS GLORY KNOWN

Exodus 7:1–6, 9:13–16

The daily news can be terrifying and depressing. From hurricanes, to shootings, to bombings, to racial and political unrest, our world is filled with catastrophes. Have you ever wondered what God's purpose is in allowing so much evil in the world? God is God! Why won't he put an end to all the violence and terror?

Our reading for today gives us a small glimpse into God's purposes in calamity. He gives Moses another intimidating assignment: Moses must again ask Pharaoh to let the Israelites go free. Moses is worried that Pharaoh won't listen to him, just as the Israelites didn't listen to the promises of God he proclaimed. Moses is also concerned that he is a man of "uncircumcised lips" (Exodus 6:12). Nevertheless, God prods him forward, telling him he is like God to Pharaoh and that his brother, Aaron, will do the talking for him.

Thus begins a series of ten horrific plagues, acts of

judgment against the Egyptians that display the power and glory of God. The first plague begins with Moses meeting Pharaoh on the bank of the Nile River. After acknowledging Pharaoh's refusal to let the Israelites go, Moses strikes the Nile with his staff and the water turns to blood. But Pharaoh's heart is hardened, and he refuses to listen. The plagues continue—frogs, gnats, flies, the death of livestock, boils, hail, locusts, darkness, and finally the Passover. A similar pattern emerges in many of the plagues: the Egyptians are afflicted, Pharaoh promises release of the Israelites in return for ending the plague, Moses keeps his end of the deal, but Pharaoh ultimately hardens his heart and does not let the Israelites go.

We might wonder what God's purpose was in sending multiple harsh judgments upon the Egyptians when he had the power to deliver the Israelites from captivity the first time. But we're reminded through God's words to Pharaoh that nothing is wasted. He has a greater purpose than what we can see on the surface.

> "For this time I will send all my plagues on you yourself, and on your servants and your people, so that you may know that there is none like me in all the earth. For by now I could have put out my hand and struck you and your people with pestilence, and you would have been cut off from the earth. But for this purpose I have raised you up, to show you my power, so that my name may be proclaimed in all the earth" (Exodus 9:14-16).

God wanted to repeatedly show the Egyptians and the Israelites that he is God! There is no one like him! Who else could turn a river into blood; cover a land with frogs, gnats, and flies; kill only the livestock of the Egyptians and not the Israelites; and drape the world in darkness? God's strength, power, and sovereignty was displayed at the beginning and end of each plague. He wanted all to see, without a doubt, the judgment that was being cast on the Egyptians for their refusal to obey his commands. Not only was God's character made apparent to the Egyptians, but as the Israelites stood by under the shelter of God's wing, their faith must have been strengthened as well.

When our own lives turn chaotic, we often become blind to God's purposes. We wonder why he has allowed our heart to ache from a broken relationship, why he permitted us to suffer from sickness or disability, or why he has let our child stray from the faith. But in all such examples, God's proclamation to the Egyptians and Israelites is true for us as well—these things take place that we would know there is none like him in all the earth.

How does this happen? As believers, it's often in the heartaches of life that we turn our eyes upward, and come to realize that all the comforts of this world mean nothing compared to a childlike trust in the good and sovereign hand of almighty God. Our wayward child, or the death of a loved one, or a national tragedy will force us to our knees, to cry out to the only One who can offer true hope and healing in our pain.

And as we cry to him, his name is exalted, and his glory is manifested through our hope and our tears.

Lord Almighty, you are a faithful, powerful, and sovereign God. As we dwell in a chaotic world, help us to see your goodness and trust your sovereign hand. There is no one like you! May your glory be proclaimed among the nations!

Reflection Questions

1. What do you learn about the character of God through the plagues he inflicted on the Egyptians?
2. What chaos or heartache in your own life is causing you to know there is no one like him? How has God ministered to you in your time of need?

5: PASSING THE BATON OF FAITH

Exodus 12:1–13:16

A handful of years ago our family was on vacation and sitting around the campfire. In between roasting marshmallows and eating gooey s'mores, we were telling stories from the past. Our then 10- and 8-year-old children surprised us by asking how Ben and I met and eventually married. As we recounted our first meeting at the county fair, my coming to faith in Christ while in college, our painful breakup, and the meeting that reunited us two years later, I realized what an opportunity our kids had just given us. Sharing with our children stories of God's faithfulness and sustaining grace in our lives helps us pass the baton of faith.

Like all great ideas, this is one God thought of long before we did! In Exodus 12 we find the momentous occasion of the Passover. God tells each household in Israel to sacrifice a lamb without blemish and put the blood on the doorposts of their houses. When the Lord passed through the land of Egypt that night, striking the firstborn, he would pass over the houses with blood

on the doorposts. God uses this very tangible teaching
style to point to the true Lamb of God who would take
away the sins of the world (John 1:29). And he wants this
memorial to be kept throughout all generations. "You
shall observe this rite as a statute for you and for your
sons forever. And when you come to the land that the
Lord will give you, as he has promised, you shall keep this
service" (Exodus 12:24-25).

After the tenth plague—the death of all the firstborn
sons in Egypt—Pharaoh was more than ready to be rid
of the Israelites. God's people were finally free after 430
years of slavery! Thus the exodus was successful, even
to the point of plundering the Egyptians of their wealth
on the way out the door (Exodus 12:36). Now God
was instructing Moses to mark this day of liberation by
celebrating a Feast of Unleavened Bread and consecrating
the firstborn of both animals and man.

The Israelites had fled Egypt in such a rush that there
had been no time to leaven their dough, so in the wilderness
they were able to bake only unleavened cakes. As a way of
remembering that hasty exit from Egypt, each year the Israelites would eat unleavened bread for seven days and then,
on the seventh day, celebrate a feast to the Lord. In addition,
as a way of remembering how God spared the Israelites
when he struck down the firstborn of all the Egyptians,
God instructed the Israelites to consecrate the firstborn of
all animals and man. A lamb was to be killed and offered as
a sacrifice for the firstborn male or for the firstborn donkey.
The clear lesson is that redemption comes through the
death of the firstborn (Exodus 13:15). Sound familiar? It

should, because the ultimate redemption for the Israelites would be the death of Christ, the Son of God and "the firstborn among many brothers" (Romans 8:29).

In designing this remembrance, God had more than the adults in mind. He knew the children would wonder why their families do these things, so he tells the Israelites, "and when in time to come your son asks you, 'What does this mean?' you shall say to him, 'By a strong hand the Lord brought us out of Egypt, from the house of slavery'" (Exodus 13:14). Earlier in the same chapter, God instructs the Israelites, "You shall tell your son on that day, 'It is because of what the Lord did for me when I came out of Egypt.' And it shall be to you as a sign on your hand and as a memorial between your eyes, that the law of the Lord may be in your mouth. For with a strong hand the Lord has brought you out of Egypt" (Exodus 13:9-10).

God doesn't want to be forgotten. He wants his faithful and mighty acts of deliverance to be remembered every time we look at our hands or open our mouths to speak. Remembering these things is both a glory to him, and a blessing to us. And what better way of passing on such faith-building memories than by telling our own children?

Think about God's mighty works in your own life. How did you come to faith in Christ? How has God provided when you've been in need? How has he sustained you when everything else in life has gone awry? Finding opportune moments to share these stories with our children highlights God's faithfulness and personal, moment-by-moment involvement in our lives.

Each year when the various children's birthdays come around, I tell them the story of going into labor with them, the exciting and surprising things that happened in those hours, and how God miraculously brought them safely into this world. It never ceases to amaze me that, even on birthdays when I've forgotten to tell them the story (or been too tired at the end of the day), they are quick to remind me: "Mom, you haven't told the story yet about how I was born." It has become a yearly tradition of remembering God's miracle of life being brought to earth. I suppose this is something they will age out of eventually, but it's a great joy to us in this season of life.

Similarly, even the simple routines of family devotions at the end of dinner, or praying in our minivan on our way to Sunday worship, are ways I hope God will stir in our children's hearts eyes of faith and praise. Your traditions don't need to be elaborate, though. Simply finding space in the everyday of life to point to God's goodness and steadfastness can do much to help pass the baton of faith to our children.

> *Lord Jesus, help us to remember the mighty works you've done in our lives. Just as the Passover reminds us of your powerful deliverance of the Israelites, help us establish traditions that remind us of your faithfulness in our own lives. Let us not neglect passing the baton of faith to our children, that your name may be praised in generations to come!*

Reflection Questions

1. What were some instances of God's mighty power that the Israelites' could share with their children?
2. How did the Passover and consecration of the firstborn demonstrate a tangible lesson about the gospel?
3. What are some simple traditions you can implement to remind your children of the goodness and faithfulness of God?

6: GOD PROVIDES A WAY OF ESCAPE

Exodus 13:17–22

As the Israelites began their journey to the Promised Land, the most direct, convenient route passed right through the heart of Philistine territory. The Philistines were brave, strong warriors who likely wanted a piece of Canaan for themselves. There would be no way the Israelites could take that route without a full-on battle. Yet the Israelites were a weary group of mostly women and children who saw themselves as victims of the Egyptian oppression. They had never traveled outside the land of Goshen, had never been trained to use weapons, and had no idea how to fight. Without a doubt they would have been crushed by the Philistines. Yet God knew all this and had compassion on them.

> When Pharaoh let the people go, God did not lead them by way of the land of the Philistines, although that was near. For God said, "Lest the people change their minds when they see war and return to Egypt." But God led the people around by the way of the wilderness toward the Red Sea (Exodus 13:17-18).

God knew that if he allowed the Israelites to go the most direct way, their confidence and trust in him would be shattered by the pummeling of the Philistines. The Israelites could easily decide that life had been more comfortable and predictable in Egypt, and want to turn back around (which is exactly what happened two years later). So in the Lord's wisdom he led them the long way to Canaan. The way of the wilderness would be a much lengthier journey, and marked by many difficulties. But God would build the Israelites' faith in him as they saw him provide water for the thirsty, food for the hungry, and protection along the way. He provided a way of escape from certain disaster, but that escape wasn't going to be a smooth-sailing, easy-peasy kind of ride.

How many times has God spared us from suffering or temptation, a trial that could very well crush our faith in him? How often do we think we can see the obvious way to accomplish our goals, yet God blocks that route and chooses a different, longer path for us, one that turns out to be marked with unwanted difficulties?

He uses these wilderness times of our life to shape us and mold us to be more like him. And when temptation or an insurmountable trial arises, he always provides a way of escape. First Corinthians 10:13 tells us, "No temptation has overtaken you that is not common to man. God is faithful, and he will not let you be tempted beyond your ability, but with the temptation he will also provide the way of escape, that you may be able to endure it."

The saying is true that God only gives us what we can handle. But not what we can handle *on our own*—what we can handle by his sustaining, enabling grace. Temptations and trials are a natural part of life. We should not be surprised when they come our way (1 Peter 4:12). But when the trial seems too much to bear, we need to cry out to the only One who can provide a way of escape.

When you've been battling the idol of food and the second piece of cheesecake is calling your name, cry out to the Lord for a way of escape. But know that often those escape routes require difficult steps of faith and action. You may need to throw the dessert in the trash, plead for grace not to give in to the lusts of the flesh, or step outside and go for a brisk walk. Maybe all three.

The way of escape is likely not the easy thing to do. Don't think of it as a shortcut or a hack, some kind of spiritual quick fix. It's typically the longer but the far better way to go.

When the temptation to wallow in self-pity and despair is at your door, sing to the Lord a new song. Ask him for grace to get out of bed and do the next thing. Look for a way to serve another in need instead of being absorbed in your own problems. God is compassionate and gracious to us in our trials. Just as he knew the Israelites could not handle battling the Philistines right off the bat on their journey, he sees us and knows our besetting sins and weaknesses.

God is eager to be the One who rescues us from difficulty. And he longs for us to cry out to him to *provide a path to freedom.*

Lord, thank you for the compassion you show us in our trials. Your ways are higher than our ways and so much better! When sin and temptation are crouching at our door, help us to cry out to you and trust you'll provide a way of escape!

Reflection Questions

1. What aspects of God's character are displayed in his choosing to take the Israelites on a longer path through the wilderness?
2. When have you seen God deliver you from a trial or temptation in an unexpected way?
3. In what area of your life do you need to trust God to provide a way of escape?

7: IDEALIZING THE PAST

Exodus 14:1–12

Have you ever noticed a tendency to look back on a previous time in your life as your golden age? As we mother school-age children, it seems life gets faster with each new school year. For my family, entering middle school has involved shuttling our teenage daughter to daily sports practice, play rehearsal, or music recitals. Although I'm thankful for the opportunities she's been given, I can find myself remembering the "simpler" days of mothering when she was at home with me all day, our main outing being a trip to the grocery store. Now it seems the Reaoch shuttle bus is running almost 24-7.

At this stage, I can easily fall into the trap of thinking things were easier and happier in the early years of mothering. But if I could rewind time, I'd likely find myself busy with diapering and potty training and keeping little ones entertained, wishing for a few minutes of peace and quiet. *Surely, things will get easier as the kids get older!* was something I remember thinking often. Reflecting on past times in life as the ideal is part of our human, sinful tendency. We're prone to be discontent, and often wish for what we do not have.

Despite the miraculous deliverance of the Israelites from Egyptian rule, they are filled with fear as they see the Egyptians pursuing them near the Red Sea. Immediately they wonder, *has God led us out of Egypt only to die?* They cry and whine and wish they were back in Egypt as slaves. This time of trial and testing causes them to idealize their former life of slavery, and they quickly lose sight of hope.

> And the people of Israel cried out to the Lord. They said to Moses, "Is it because there are no graves in Egypt that you have taken us away to die in the wilderness? What have you done to us in bringing us out of Egypt? Is not this what we said to you in Egypt: 'Leave us alone that we may serve the Egyptians'? For it would have been better for us to serve the Egyptians than to die in the wilderness." (Exodus 14:10b-12)

Their present hardship is causing them to forget the chains they were in just days earlier. They're forgetting the forced labor, their treatment as possessions rather than people, their inability to choose where to live or work, and they're ready to blame Moses for all their current problems.

The danger of letting our minds dwell on the past is that we can gloss over the trials we were experiencing then and paint in our minds a picture-perfect ideal. Like the Israelites, we are prone to think that trading today's problems for yesterday's would erase our unhappiness and dissatisfaction. Instead we need to trust that the Lord, who knows our every need, is worthy to be trusted in whatever situation he currently has us in. It's a matter of contentment, a matter of choosing to bloom where he has planted us.

When you find yourself daydreaming about a former time in your life that you wish you could go back to, fix your mind on these truths about God's character.

1. **God is good.** This simple fact is a poignant reminder that he is worthy to be trusted. God is for us and not against us. Whatever problem you may be dealing with, remember the goodness of God, in both the happy times and the bad.
2. **God is sovereign.** Nothing catches God by surprise. He knew and ordained that the Israelites would be pursued by the Egyptians at the Red Sea. He created your inmost being. He knows the very hairs on our heads. And he ordains whatever circumstances we find ourselves currently walking through. Much peace can be experienced when we trust the goodness and sovereignty of God.
3. **God is faithful.** He will never leave you or forsake you. He is faithful to keep his promises. And he promises to use all things for the good of those who love him, who have been called by his purpose (Romans 8:28).

Father, give us thankful hearts and keep us from looking at the past with rose-colored glasses. Let our ultimate satisfaction be found in you instead of our imagined ideal circumstances. Help us to choose to bloom where you've planted us.

Reflection Questions

1. What evidences of God's faithfulness should the Israelites have turned to when they were gripped with fear?
2. What seasons of your life do you find yourself idealizing? How can you choose to trust God and bloom where he has planted you?

8: THE LORD WILL FIGHT FOR YOU

Exodus 14:13–30

A dear friend of mine in ministry shared with me how she and her husband had been maligned by someone in leadership at their church. Due to theological disagreements, they had decided to leave the church, where they had served for many years. But as they started to visit new churches in their small city, they quickly learned that the pastors of these churches had been warned of their "divisiveness," so they were not warmly welcomed. When her husband applied to a ministry internship program in another state, he was rejected because of a bad report from this same person.

With every bone in her body my friend wanted to scream the truth, to describe what had happened in their church to cause the relational fracture, and to defend herself and her husband. But a mentor advised her to be quiet, pray, and wait for the Lord, the avenger who will fight for us. How difficult this can be when we're being persecuted or slandered! We want to prove the other person wrong. We want to defend ourselves so that no one thinks badly of us. But sometimes, being silent and letting the truth prevail is exactly what we should do.

Can you imagine the fear the Israelites felt as they saw the massive Egyptian army coming toward them at top speed? They desperately needed protection. In their panic and fear they wished they were back in Egypt, living as slaves. Their understandable terror filled their thinking with idealistic visions of the past. Surely they felt utterly helpless to defend themselves against such a great and powerful army. With no military training and no familiarity with the area, they believed their lives would soon end. But God in his mercy had a different plan.

> And Moses said to the people, "Fear not, stand firm, and see the salvation of the Lord, which he will work for you today. For the Egyptians whom you see today, you shall never see again. The Lord will fight for you, and you have only to be silent." (Exodus 14:13-14)

When their every instinct was preparing them for fight or flight, the Lord was telling them to be still and confidently watch him work. He would be their defender. They didn't need military might. They didn't even need to open their mouths. No cries of fear were needed, no screams of defense. "You have only to be silent," said Moses (Exodus 14:14). Being still and quiet in the face of a fierce attack demonstrates trust in God. It's like putting down our toy cap gun because we know the tanks will arrive at any moment.

And in a miracle only God could do, he instructed Moses to stretch his hand over the sea and God drove back the waters, allowing the Israelites to walk across on dry ground. When the Israelites arrived safely at the other side, their Egyptian enemies pursued them full-force into the seabed, but again God had Moses stretch out his hand. The waters broke in on the Egyptians, throwing them into a panic and burying their chariots and horsemen under an overwhelming flood.

God's omnipotent power and sovereignty over this situation was shown through his confident commands to the Israelites (Exodus 14:13-14), followed by his actions. He is a comforter, offering peace to the fearful. He invited the Israelites to rest in himself, the source of salvation. He offered hope through the promise they would never see the Egyptians again. And he is actively working for us, today, as we face our own "fighting without and fear within" (2 Corinthians 7:5).

My friends whose reputation had been marred quietly waited for the truth to prevail as they continued doing good and seeking God's will. The following year the husband was accepted into the ministry internship program that had first rejected him. Eventually he was offered a ministry position at that very church. God has since blessed them with decades of fruitful ministry. Instead of rushing to defend themselves by sharing their side of the story with anyone who would listen, they allowed the Lord to fight for them. And God honored their trust and humility.

How often do we feel the need to run ahead of God? When have you taken matters into your own hands and assumed the role of divine avenger? It can be tempting every time a snarky remark is made on social media, or someone says something that casts you in a bad light. Or maybe you have worked hard in hopes of getting a promotion at work, yet someone else is picked for the job. Do you want to let your boss and coworkers know the unfairness of the situation, or why the other person is less qualified than you?

Our natural, sinful temptation is to return evil for evil and give the offending person a taste of his own medicine. But God reminds us that there is a better way. Although there is a time to stand for justice and truth, there are also many times when we need to leave matters in God's hands, to let him do the fighting for us. Often our best fighting happens on our knees.

Thank you, Lord, that you are our avenger! Keep us from the temptation to take matters into our own hands and repay evil with evil. Help us to trust that you will fight for us.

Reflection Questions

1. How do these verses provide hope and comfort to you?
2. What is a situation in your life that would be better fought by putting your weapons down and letting the Lord fight for you?

9: VACATIONS DON'T LAST FOREVER

Exodus 15:22–16:3

Each summer, our family of six loads our minivan full of suitcases, beach toys, coolers, and towels, and drives seven hours north to a picturesque town on the coast of Lake Huron. All of us look forward to this yearly tradition. My husband enjoys a break from his responsibilities at church. I enjoy a respite from the cooking, cleaning, and laundry that typically fills my days. And our kids enjoy much more of our undivided attention and the fun of the water and sand.

There are hardly any "have-to's" during that week, which is part of what makes it so gloriously relaxing. Each day we just peer out the window to decide whether it is a better day for swimming or putt-putt golf or board games. In a way the clock seems to stop, and we enjoy the gift of rest in a way that can seem impossible at home.

But vacations don't last forever. And in a week's time there is a mountain of laundry that needs to be done, responsibilities at church and home that need to be attended to, and all those calendar reminders that keep popping up on our phones.

Throughout the Israelites' difficult trek through the wilderness, there were some mountaintop, vacation-type experiences, too—but many more low valleys and hardships through which they needed to persevere. In Exodus 15, after Moses and the Israelites rejoice over the victory at the crossing of the Red Sea, God again takes them through a valley. They enter the wilderness of Shur, and for three days find no water (Exodus 15:22). And when the parched Israelites finally do find water at Marah, it is bitter, undrinkable.

Again the Israelites grumble and complain. But God is merciful, showing Moses a log that will make the water sweet. The Lord reminds them of the blessings of obedience (Exodus 15:26), telling them that if they listen diligently to his voice and keep his commands, he'll protect them from diseases that the Egyptians suffered. And then, to top off his promise of a blessing, God leads them to the oasis of Elim.

After wandering for three days, parched by thirst, the Israelites must have felt like they were in heaven when they saw twelve springs of water and seventy palm trees where they could set up camp. These precious gifts were surely received with eager hearts—a time of rest, shade, and relaxation after a dry trek through the desert. There among Elim's luxuries, God was giving his people not just encouragement and refreshment, but an opportunity to rest and ponder his exhortation about keeping his commands. Like all earthly rests, however, this vacation came to an end.

It may have seemed to the Israelites like they had hardly arrived at Elim when it was time to pack up and set out on the next leg of their journey. And soon Moses and Aaron again faced a whiny, hungry horde, wishing they were back in Egypt where the meat pots were full and the bread plentiful.

Have you ever wondered why God doesn't allow our mountaintop experiences to last very long? I know that, at least in my case, I don't normally see my need for Christ very clearly when I'm on vacation. Laying on the beach, sipping lemonade, at the all-inclusive resort (or at least someplace a lot more relaxing than home), I have to remind myself that this is not heaven on earth. Yet God often uses those times to revive us and give us a fresh sense of gratitude.

It's in the valleys of life, when food is scarce, or anxieties are mounting, that I sense my greatest need for Jesus. It is in the low times that I am desperate for a glimmer of hope from his Word. It's in those moments that I cry out to him for help and sustaining grace. It's not that God doesn't want us to enjoy life's vacations, but he knows all too well that our dependence on him will decrease if we receive only blessing and no hardship. We will be powerfully tempted to become self-reliant and forgetful of all he has done. But God is glorified when we cry out to him for help and salvation. He reminds us in these desert times of life that he is our rock and our fortress, our provider and our salvation.

So if you happen to find yourself in a "vacation" spot today, be thankful for this gift. Be refreshed and ponder all the ways God has been faithful to bless you. And for those of you in a valley, remember that these are the times God is using to refine you and to strengthen you, as you learn to depend on him more and more.

Father God, help us to have grateful hearts for the restful, "vacation" times of life. But also help us to be thankful for the valleys, when our need for you is often more apparent. Teach us to trust you and depend on you, no matter what season of life we're in.

Reflection Questions
1. Why doesn't God let our mountaintop experiences last?
2. Are you in a "vacation" time of life right now, or a difficult valley? How can you see God at work in whatever season you're in?
3. How can you be grateful despite your circumstances?

10: THE CURSE OF COMPLAINING

Exodus 16:2–8

How do you react when something doesn't go your way? I've noticed how even when I'm on cloud nine after a mountaintop experience—whether a conference, retreat, or vacation—all it takes is some small annoyance and a fountain of complaints begin spewing from my mouth.

You're leaving your women's conference singing fresh worship songs when someone cuts you off in traffic. "I can't believe the nerve of that person!" You receive good news of your husband's raise at work and you're thanking the Lord—but the next day you feel depressed by an unexpected medical bill that takes it all back. One minute you're praising your children for a job well done at school, and the next you're filled with frustration that they made a mess in the kitchen again. "Haven't I told you a hundred times to throw away your trash and put your dishes in the dishwasher!?" How quickly our fickle hearts are exposed by our words.

In Exodus 16 the Israelites had just come from a mountaintop experience. After wandering in the wilder-

ness for three days without any water, God had led them
to the desert resort of Elim. In Elim there was plenty of
water and the shade of 70 palm trees to cool their hot and
wearied bodies. But just after they left Elim they entered
the wilderness of Sin. Complaints poured from their
mouths as their stomachs rumbled with hunger. They
quickly focused their whining on the two men who were
leading them, Moses and Aaron.

> And the whole congregation of the people of Israel
> grumbled against Moses and Aaron in the wilderness,
> and the people of Israel said to them, "Would that we
> had died by the hand of the Lord in the land of Egypt,
> when we sat by the meat pots and ate bread to the
> full, for you have brought us out into this wilderness
> to kill this whole assembly with hunger" (Exodus
> 16:2-3).

Again the Israelites were caught in the trap of idealizing the past; it's amazing how hungry stomachs can sour
our words. Their days of slavery suddenly looked like
days of feasting. The Israelites even suspected that Moses
and Aaron were trying to kill them with hunger!

Yet God in his mercy heard the complaints of his
people. He was not detached or ignorant of their needs,
but provided a generous solution. Each day he would rain
bread from heaven, which the Israelites named manna,
and they were to collect only enough for a day's portion.
Moreover, on the sixth day, they were to collect and
prepare twice as much so they could rest on the Sabbath,

when no manna would appear. In this magnificent display of provision, God was not only providing for his people but testing their obedience to him. He was showing the Israelites that he is the Lord who brought them up out of Egypt and that he hears their grumbling (Exodus 16:4-7). He was also teaching them daily dependence on him, his promises, and his life-sustaining provision.

Ultimately, this dependence and provision points to trusting in Jesus, the true "bread of God" who came from heaven (John 6:31-35). In God's instructions about the collection of manna we see a pattern of work and rest laid out for us by the Lord of the universe, a pattern that will give us much blessing and peace when we follow it, rather than imagining that our own way is better.

After all, when something in our life goes awry and we do voice our complaints, who are we really directing them towards? In Exodus 16:8, Moses rebukes the Israelites, because their complaints against him and his brother are ultimately against God.

"When the Lord gives you in the evening meat to eat and in the morning bread to the full, because the Lord has heard your grumbling that you grumble against him— what are we? Your grumbling is not against us but against the Lord."

Sometimes we do the same sort of thing, don't we? We get frustrated with the clerk at the store who rang our items up wrong, and correct her with a less than gentle and kind tone of voice. We get annoyed that our kids are disrupting our work again by constant requests for snacks, and we lash out at them. Or we quietly murmur to our coworkers about the seemingly bad decision the boss just made. In all these situations, we need to remember the One who is sovereign over every interruption and unsavory circumstance in our lives. We can pray for the Lord to guard our mouths from making the same mistake as the Israelites.

Lord, let us be a people of thankful lips, in every situation seeing your goodness and provision.

Reflection Questions

1. How do you typically respond when an expectation is not met in your life?
2. Where are you tempted to shift blame when things are not going the way you'd like?
3. What lessons can we learn from the Israelites' example?

11: THE LORD WILL PROVIDE

Exodus 16:9–20

Growing up, each Halloween my brother, sister, and I would don our costumes and carry our plastic pumpkins through the neighborhood until they were filled to the brim with candy. Once we were home we counted our pieces and secreted them away in well-marked bags in an effort to prevent unauthorized "sharing." Somehow, whether due to my appetite or for some other reason, my candy always seemed to disappear twice as fast as my sister's—who by Easter still had stale candy in her bag! My real point, however, is that sharing of treats wasn't a strength for my siblings and me. Every Halloween we turned into hoarders.

The Israelites, of course, had much more serious concerns than whether someone had made off with a few miniature Snickers bars. They were several million people marching through the wilderness, and needed a huge quantity of daily bread just to survive. And despite God's repeated provision, they continually questioned his ability or willingness to provide for them. Their response was not too different from that of my siblings and me after Halloween: selfish, fearful hoarding.

After leaving Elim, the Israelites first accused Moses and Aaron of trying to kill them with hunger, imagining that back in Egypt, as slaves, they had been able to eat as much as they liked (Exodus 16:3). But despite their grumbling the Lord was gracious and merciful to them and produced manna, raining bread from heaven each morning. He wanted this abundant provision to once again demonstrate to them who he was: "Then you shall know that I am the Lord your God" (Exodus 16:12).

Yet this provision also came with instructions that tested their faith. Each morning, five days a week, they were to gather food for that day, and on the sixth day they were to gather twice as much so they could rest on the Sabbath (Exodus 16:4-5). In addition, God perfectly provided so that no matter how much or how little one gathered, no one was left hungry. Moses also specifically instructed them not to save any of it for the morning. But for some, their sinful hearts just couldn't take God at his word. Some of them disobeyed, hoarding some manna until morning, only to find it reeking and filled with worms (Exodus 16:18-21)—even less appetizing than hard, stale candy well past its expiration date.

Aren't we often just like the Israelites? When our daily comforts are pressed, we quickly get bent out of shape and become laser-focused on our own needs. When money is tight, we begin planning how to cut corners.

Maybe we'll give less to missions, cut back on gifts, or rationalize a lack of hospitality. Hoarding of our money and possessions begins to make sense.

In these seasons, worry can consume our thoughts and affections, robbing us of precious sleep and tender care for others. We become hoarders of our time and energy. We put up boundaries that block others from being able to ask us for help, and we avoid people who we see as more likely to drain our personal reserves. It can become easy to stop trusting in God's promise to meet all our needs and give us grace for every good work to which we're called. And when we refuse to follow his plan for our provision, all we have left is our own plan—by morning rotted with the worms of pain and discouragement.

This wilderness example of God's daily provision for our needs points us to the true Bread of Life, Jesus (John 6:31-35), the ultimate source of satisfaction. Just as the Israelites looked to God to provide food to strengthen and sustain their bodies, so we look to Jesus for grace and hope in our daily lives. He is the fuel that keeps us living and working in a world that is not our home, reminding us of our glorious future.

The daily bread that fell from heaven, to be gathered and consumed one day at a time, is a reminder of our daily need to go to the Word of God for strength and wisdom. When we feed ourselves each day with the true Bread of Life, each day we have more fresh manna to share with others. We feel no need to hoard, only a desire to give life to those around us. We trust that all we have, whether spiritual blessings or earthly goods, is a gift from God. Being content with God's perfect provision frees us to give to others as he has given to us.

> Your abundance at the present time should supply their need, so that their abundance may supply your need, that there may be fairness. As it is written, "Whoever gathered much had nothing left over, and whoever gathered little had no lack." (2 Corinthians 8:14-15)

Lord Jesus, help us to trust your perfect provision in all things. You are the Bread of Life who fills our every need! Free us from being hoarders of our earthly gifts. Let us be generous with our time, money, and spiritual blessings, trusting in your abundant provision.

Reflection Questions

1. Are you looking to Jesus to provide for your needs, both physical and spiritual? If not, how are you being led astray?
2. How does your checkbook and calendar reflect your trust, or lack of trust, in God?
3. How does the Lord's daily provision of food for the Israelites point to Christ?

12: HOLD UP MY ARMS

Exodus 17:8–16

"We just can't seem to find a church that fits us," said a friend of mine. She went on to explain that, whatever church they visited, typically the worship music wasn't their style, or the preaching was too long, or some other factor made it a "bad fit." Besides, she reminded me, Sunday was their family's only "down-time." Although she considers herself a born-again Christian, and had attended Christian schools her whole life, their family simply doesn't attend church.

Our children's sports activities have given us interesting opportunities for conversation with other parents. Seated there on the sidelines in our folding chairs, small talk can easily turn to sharing bits about our lives. Although I've learned not to lead with the fact that my husband is a pastor (it turns out that's a great way to kill conversation) small talk inevitably leads to where our family is from, why we live in the area, and (eventually) the church we're a part of.

Alongside those soccer fields and track stands, I've

been surprised how open people can be about their own church experiences. And I've been troubled to meet so many professing believers, including some previously in full-time ministry, who seem to lack all commitment to a church body. "We have church in our living room with our family," said one mom.

The Christian life is not meant to be lived alone. We need each other to fight the fight of faith, hold each other accountable, remind one another of the truths of God's Word, and spur each other on to love and good deeds. Without fellow believers in our lives, we are vulnerable to being "hardened by the deceitfulness of sin" (Hebrews 3:13). We can begin to coast through life, justifying to ourselves the ungodly decisions we're making because there's no one to help us admit what's really going on. Soon our lives begin to reflect more and more the pagan society that surrounds us.

Influences from the world can be subtle. When we're not regularly sitting under faithful preaching of the Word in a local church, we can easily lose sight of the standard of truth and righteousness that helps us live in ways that are pleasing to God. Before long it can seem perfectly reasonable to sleep in on Sundays (after all, you've worked hard all week), criticize your husband in front of your coworkers, make no time to study the Bible, and pretend that TV or internet preaching is a perfectly good substitute for the live pulpit. We may claim to be Christians, but do our lives look all that different from those of our unbelieving neighbors?

In Exodus 17, Moses learned firsthand the importance of having other believers in his life. On their way to the Promised Land, the Amalekites showed up to fight with Israel. Moses took his stand on the top of a hill, staff in hand. When he raised up his hand, Israel prevailed, but whenever he lowered his hand, Amalek prevailed. As the battle raged on, Moses began to tire and needed the help of Aaron and Hur.

> But Moses' hands grew weary, so they took a stone and put it under him, and he sat on it, while Aaron and Hur held up his hands, one on one side, and the other on the other side. So his hands were steady until the going down of the sun. And Joshua overwhelmed Amalek and his people with the sword. (Exodus 17:12-13)

In God's providence, he granted victory in this case by means of a team effort. Moses' own frail humanity made it impossible for him to keep his arms in the air indefinitely. He needed his friends' help, the steadying strength of their own hands holding up his. With two faithful men beside him, victory was ensured and the Israelites were able to continue their journey.

We are not meant to be lone-ranger Christians. Life is hard, and when we try to live it on our own, without a community of faith to help hold up our arms, defeat is inevitable. Maybe you've been hurt by the church. Maybe you feel embittered toward your church leaders. Can I encourage you not to give up? The church is a place for hurting, broken people. No one is perfect. We will sin against each other and leave wounds, but don't let this be a reason to walk away and try to live the Christian life on your own.

Let's let our attitudes be like that of Christ, who freely forgave and extended grace and mercy to those who hurt him most. Commit to a body of believers and look for ways to both hold up the arms of your brothers and sisters in Christ beside you, as well as be held up by them. Giving and receiving in a church body is a two-way street. You need the church just as much as they need you.

Heavenly Father, thank you for the gift of the body of Christ! Help us to be committed to a local body of believers, willing to both give and receive the help and accountability we need to live the Christian life.

Reflection Questions

1. Are you trying to live the Christian life on your own, or are you committed to a body of believers? Why or why not?
2. In what ways have you experienced having other believers in Christ hold up your arms?
3. What are some of the dangers of being a lone-ranger Christian?

13: THE LAW LEADS US TO GRACE

Exodus 20:1–21

Decorating the house for Christmas is something our whole family looks forward to. We usually start first thing in the morning, bringing out the boxes of lights and ornaments and figurines, delighting over the sentimental treasures that will soon adorn our home. Christmas music plays as we string lights on a freshly cut tree. It's typically a precious family time that we all treasure. But one year in particular, someone put a damper on the fun.

I walked into the living room, where our four children were gathered, to find our 2-year-old son unwrapping a box of expensive, delicate ornaments we'd brought back from a special family vacation. I admonished him and put the box in a spot he couldn't reach. Minutes later, I came back into the room to find the same box back on the floor, my then 2-year-old son about to pull the arm off his older brother's beloved Captain Hook, and my 7-year-old daughter standing there watching! I wish I could say I responded calmly. But my annoyance and impatience turned to anger as I yelled out, "Who gave him the special ornaments?!" I grabbed the box from the floor and thrust it onto an even higher shelf, indignant at the seeming irresponsibility of my children.

Suddenly everything changed, and the joy went out of the room. My kids looked at me with tear-filled eyes, startled and ashamed by my anger. The happy Christmas music sounded very out of place.

Remorse instantly filled my heart. Within minutes I knew I needed to apologize to each of my children. It can be hard to say I'm sorry and seek forgiveness, especially for a sinful reaction to something that legitimately needed correcting. But my sin was still sin. So as Captain Hook looked on, both arms still fully attached, I swallowed my pride and asked the kids to forgive me for my outburst. "This is why Mom needs Jesus."

Acknowledging our sin to others has a unique way of pointing us back to our Savior. When we humble ourselves by seeking Christ's forgiveness, as well as the forgiveness of others, we're owning our imperfection and looking to the only perfect one, the only one who can cleanse us and refresh our sin-saturated souls. Sin is a reminder that, try as we might, we're completely unable to fulfill God's commands perfectly. It's the words of his law that point us to our need for grace.

In Exodus 20 we encounter one of the most famous passages in all of Scripture—the giving of the Ten Commandments. The Lord descends on Mount Sinai in fire and calls Moses to come meet with him. In typical fashion, he reminds the Israelites who he is before addressing how they should live. "I am the Lord your God, who brought you out of the land of Egypt, out of the house of slavery" (Exodus 20:2). Perhaps, before giving them rules for their daily lives, he wanted to invoke his authority and remind them of his power to deliver them from their oppressors. In these famous commandments God addresses idolatry, taking his name in vain, the Sabbath, honoring parents, murder, adultery, stealing, lying, and coveting. These commands, indeed all of God's commands, are given to us for our own good and for his glory.

If everyone kept God's laws, can you imagine what the world would be like? But the truth of the matter is that in our sin-born state none of us can keep the law. No matter how hard we try, we are bound to mess up. Romans 3:23 tells us, "For all have sinned and fall short of the glory of God." Other than Jesus Christ, there are no perfect people. Certainly as believers in Christ we have the power to fight sin and temptation through the Holy Spirit who lives inside of us. But for as long as we live on this earth, we will never be without failure. And it is the commands of God that show us how miserably we fail, revealing to us our need for a Savior, a rescuer from sin.

Our hope does not lie in ourselves or our performance. We cannot gain God's blessing through obeying his commands, and we can't do enough good deeds to earn forgiveness for even the smallest sin. Our hope is solely in what Christ has already done, what he accomplished for us on the cross.

Our righteousness will never come from being good enough. It comes from Christ, who granted us new life in himself and placed trust in our hearts—trust in the one atoning death that covers all our sin. Second Corinthians 5:21 tells us, "For our sake he made him to be sin who knew no sin, so that in him we might become the righteousness of God." Every day, each time we fail to keep God's perfect commands, what glorious assurance we can have, knowing that our righteousness is not in anything that we do, but in Christ alone. When we fail, when we sin, amidst the remorse and regret we can thank God for his commandments, for they reveal our imperfections and lead us to the cross, our only hope of ever being counted good enough.

Thank you, Jesus, that your blood has covered all our sins! Thank you that our failure to keep your perfect commands reveals our need for a Savior. May we find our righteousness in You alone.

Reflection Questions
1. How does the world see the Ten Commandments? How do you see them?
2. How does God's law lead us to grace? How do you see the gospel presented through the Ten Commandments?

14: THE LORD DWELLS AMONG US

Exodus 25:1–9

I'm going on about year 14 of sleep deprivation. Having four children over a 10-year span has meant that, for most years, one child or another has been regularly waking up in the middle of the night. Our youngest child has had the most difficult time. Although he's finally improving, many nights I'm still awakened by "Mommy! Mommy!" When I stumble half asleep into his room, he often tells me he's scared and wants me to stay beside him. In my sleepy voice I remind our little guy of God's constant presence. "You're not alone, Micah. Who is here with you? Who can you call to when you're scared?" "Jesus!" he replies with confidence. "Jesus is with me."

As believers in Christ we can be sure that Jesus is with us. He dwells within our hearts through the third person of the Trinity, the Holy Spirit. And through the Holy Spirit, God guides us, gives us wisdom, reminds us of his words, and convicts us of our sin. But in the days of Moses, God chose a different way to dwell with his people.

Exodus 25-30 is the story of God instructing his people about a tabernacle where his presence will dwell, an elaborate tent containing two separate spaces and several pieces of furniture, including the ark of the covenant, a golden lampstand, and more. In extreme detail God instructs them about the tabernacle itself — the building materials and the dimensions of the furniture. He also details how the priests of the tabernacle will be chosen, how they will perform daily sacrifices, and how God will meet his people there.

This tabernacle, the place for meeting with God, would be packed up and carried with the Israelites throughout their wilderness journey. Each day, God guided them using a pillar of cloud by day and a pillar of fire by night. When the cloud settled in one spot, that's where the tabernacle was to be erected, with the people camped around it, all of them remaining there until the cloud moved on. Just as God's Word guides us in our daily lives, God was providing a tangible way to lead his people.

The specificity of God's tabernacle instructions reminds us that we must never try to follow him on our own terms or by our own methods. He is our Lord and God; we do not belong to ourselves. How we are to live comes from his gracious instructions, given for our good and that of our families and churches. God did not depend on Moses for the tabernacle's master plan, but instead demanded, "Exactly as I show you concerning the pattern of the tabernacle, and of all its furniture, so you shall make it" (Exodus 25:9). Through his detailed instructions, God showed Israel that worship must be by his own design.

How thankful we can be that God did not leave us
without instruction for how to worship and honor him
with our lives! Instead, he provided us with the living
and active Word of God that has the power to convict
us of sin and transform our minds. The culture tells us
we can create our own gods and make up the rules we
want to live by. After all, they say, isn't the Bible outdated
in its beliefs about sex, homosexuality, and the roles of
husbands and wives? But to buy into those cultural lies is
to lose the standard of holiness God has given us for our
own blessing and joy. It is to forfeit the full power of the
promise found in Exodus 20:4-6, that we will be shown
steadfast love from the Lord when we choose to keep his
commandments.

Where the Israelites had the tabernacle, we have
something so much greater: God dwelling with us and
within us. John 1:14 tells us "the Word became flesh and
dwelt among us." Jesus Christ came to tabernacle among
us. He came to earth and lived a perfect life, and his bodily
sacrifice set us free from the punishment we rightly
deserve for our sin.

Unlike the priests who had to make daily atonement
for the sins of the people, Jesus made a single atoning
sacrifice, once for all. "He has no need, like those high
priests, to offer sacrifices daily, first for his own sins and
then for those of the people, since he did this once for
all when he offered up himself" (Hebrews 7:27). His

own body was the dwelling place of God that would be destroyed and raised (John 2:19-21). Then, by his ascension and the outpouring of the Holy Spirit, he came to dwell within us. He is the cornerstone on which the church is built (Ephesians 2:20), and God's Spirit dwells in the heart of each and every believer in Christ.

How often do you dwell on the amazing fact that God is with us? That he is dwelling in our souls? In the busyness of life we can often forget to meditate on this wondrous truth. Cry out to the One who can lead you and guide you and help you in this wilderness of life. And soak up the truths of his Word—your own pillar of cloud that will direct your steps each day.

Father God, thank you that you are always with us. Thank you that you did not leave us without instruction, but gifted us with the truth of your Word. May we be diligent to seek your wisdom each day.

Reflection Questions

1. How does the tabernacle foreshadow the coming of Christ?
2. In what areas of life do you need to remind yourself that God is with you? That he is able to guide you and help you?

15: LOVING DIFFICULT PEOPLE

Exodus 32:1–14

It was only a three-minute escape. If I told you that my name was being chanted that entire time, over and over, louder and louder, with growing urgency, along with pounding on the door, you might think I'm a pop star or film icon.

But no. I was simply the mother of a toddler who thought he could only be content in my arms. And my escape? An unglamorous trip to the bathroom, a chance to take a deep breath behind a locked door before reentering that world of diapers, blocks, and Daniel Tiger. Because, even though I loved this little guy with all my heart, at times he could be a difficult person to keep showing love to, especially in the midst of his tantrums and tears.

Can you think of a difficult person in your own life? It's probably not hard. In our broken, sin-filled world, they are everywhere. The co-worker willing to do anything to get ahead, including taking credit for your ideas. The in-laws who always seem to be peering over your shoulder, critiquing your parenting skills, and offering "suggestions" for improvement. The child who knows exactly how to push your buttons, leaving you exasperated and flustered again. The person in your ministry who constantly complains about your leadership, who thinks he has better ideas and communicates them with a sharp and biting tongue. The passive-aggressive friend who is kind one moment and gives you the cold shoulder the next. The list can go on and on.

What do we do with these people? With constant strained relationships? Our natural tendency is to run the other way, to simply avoid them. But is that what honors God in these hard situations?

Moses was no stranger to dealing with difficult people. Even after rescuing them out of slavery and leading them safely away from the Egyptians, the Israelites were far from happy with him. Instead of being grateful for their new freedom and provision from God, they shed tears over the menu (Numbers 11:4-6), grumbled about not having water (Numbers 20:2-3), wished they had died in Egypt, and wanted to choose another leader willing to march them back into slavery! (Numbers 14:2-4). Even Moses's own siblings were jealous of his leadership and complained about their brother and his non-Israelite wife (Numbers 12:1-2).

Yet what amazes me about Moses is that he didn't retaliate against this annoying group of people. He didn't even defend himself. Instead, he demonstrated amazing humility and compassion toward those he led, repeatedly interceding for them. Moses was a foreshadow of Christ, our Intercessor who gives us grace upon grace, extending mercy to the vilest of sinners.

At the start of Exodus 32 the Israelites have become impatient waiting for Moses to return from Mount Sinai. Sadly, they seem to have forgotten all that God has accomplished for them, along with his decrees, as they ask Aaron to make a false god for them to follow as they continue on their journey. "Up, make us gods who shall go before us. As for this Moses, the man who brought us up out of the land of Egypt, we do not know what has become of him" (Exodus 32:1). And much to our dismay, the brother of Moses, the co-leader of this wilderness journey, readily agrees to the wicked endeavor and begins collecting jewelry to create a golden calf to worship.

Meanwhile, God tells Moses to return to this adulterous people as his anger burns hot against them. God is ready to wipe the Israelites out as they blatantly defy his commands (Exodus 32:10). And really, Moses has every reason to agree with God. They have been difficult and disobedient from the very start of the journey, constantly finding things to whine about, and repeatedly criticizing Moses' leadership. Surprisingly, Moses begs the Lord to relent.

> "O Lord, why does your wrath burn hot against your
> people, whom you have brought out of the land of
> Egypt with great power and with a mighty hand?
> Why should the Egyptians say, 'With evil intent did

he bring them out, to kill them in the mountains and
to consume them from the face of the earth'? Turn
from your burning anger and relent from this disaster
against your people." (Exodus 32:11-12)

Moses appeals in the hope that God's name will not
be defamed by the Egyptians. He desires that God's name
continue to be glorified among the nations. In the parallel
account at Deuteronomy 9:18 we see him lying prostrate
before the Lord, fasting and praying for 40 days and
nights on behalf of these rebellious, disobedient, ungrateful people. And God listens to Moses. He relents from his
initial plan, and spares the people of Israel (Exodus 32:14).

What a powerful example Moses provides us, of continuing to love a hard-to-love and defiant group of people. He
never stopped caring for the Israelites, even at their worst.
And we too, by the grace of God, can demonstrate love
and concern for the difficult people God places in our
own lives. When we are tempted to throw in the towel on
our own strained relationships, let us follow the example
of Moses and cry out to the Lord for mercy — to soften
our own hearts and the hearts of those we struggle with.
If we have truly forgiven those who have wronged us, we
should be able to pray for God's mercy and blessing upon
them. We who have been forgiven freely should extend
that same lavish grace to those who have hurt us. And let's
not forget that we may be the difficult person in someone
else's life!

So when that child has you on the brink of tears, or you've just received a harsh and critical email about your ministry, or you're confronted with that extended family member who drives you up the wall, ask God for grace not to run away, but to keep on loving that hard-to-love person.

God will be honored and our hearts will find deeper satisfaction as we seek to love people just as Christ loved us when we were his enemies.

Lord Jesus, help us to persevere in loving the difficult people in our lives. Forgive us for those times when we want to quit and walk away. Give us the grace to love others the way you love us—with abundant mercy, patience, and kindness.

Reflection Questions

1. In what ways does Moses show us how to love difficult people?
2. Who are the difficult people in your life? How can you move toward them in love, giving grace the way the Lord has given grace to you?

16: THE GRASS ISN'T GREENER

Numbers 11:1–17

Getting a watch battery replaced was the one errand I had for the day. On a cold, snowy morning, a short visit to the mall seemed like a good use of my time. I could get my watch running again and take my energetic toddler to the play area for a bit. Although we live about five minutes from one of the nicest malls in our area, I avoid it as much as possible. It's just not good for my soul. Whenever I set foot in the place, I realize how many things I "need." Enticing window displays, shiny leather shoes, the latest fashions, giant red SALE signs—I'm like a moth drawn to flame.

All of a sudden I realize how dingy my boots look, how out of style my coat is, and why I had better jump on this clearance sale before it's gone. Things I had been content with ten minutes earlier now urgently need to be replaced. Discontent sets in, leading me down a steep path toward a host of other sins.

The Israelites weren't familiar with malls, but they were intimately familiar with the slippery slope of discontentment. Their long trek through the wilderness and their craving for tastier food led to a barrage of complaints. It seems preposterous that people could look back on their recent slavery as a time of abundance and goodness, but that's exactly what the Israelites did. It's the kind of thing discontentment can do to us, too, causing us to idealize our past and despise the blessings of the present.

Although God had miraculously delivered the Israelites out of slavery, their limited menu options in the wilderness led them to tears as they longed for the food they had eaten in Egypt. "And the people of Israel also wept again and said, 'Oh that we had meat to eat! We remember the fish we ate in Egypt that cost nothing, the cucumbers, the melons, the leeks, the onions, and the garlic'" (Numbers 11:4-5). It seems they didn't remember the food was only "free" in Egypt because they had been slaves! The "grass is greener" syndrome blinded them from seeing the goodness of God, who had led them out of slavery and was now miraculously meeting their needs in the wilderness.

Manna from heaven, pillars of cloud and fire guiding their way, water from stone (we'll cover that later in this book): daily miracles, daily provision. Yet Numbers 11 tells us the people of God complained.

One whiny voice sharing its woes with another lights a fire that spreads quickly. All of a sudden everyone is focused on what's wrong with a situation instead of what's right. I think back to my days teaching elementary school. When I told the class it was time to clean up the craft and get out their math books, all it took was one student to let out a moan, and in two seconds half the class was joining in.

Complaining is contagious. The Israelites' whining infected Moses, leading him down a path of self-pity (Numbers 11:11-14). Overwhelmed and burdened by their requests for meat, Moses told God he'd rather die than deal with the ungrateful Israelites. "If you will treat me like this, kill me at once, if I find favor in your sight, that I may not see my wretchedness" (Numbers 11:15). The discontent that had led to complaining now produced despair. Thankfully, the Lord heard Moses' cry and had compassion on him. He didn't judge Moses for his desperate plea, but instead provided 70 elders to shoulder the load of leading and shepherding the Israelites, "and they shall bear the burden of the people with you, so that you may not bear it yourself alone" (Numbers 11:17).

We should never be afraid to disclose our true feelings to the Lord. God will meet us where we're at. Our discontentment, complaining, ingratitude, and idealizing of the past all point to a deeper root from which these ugly sins sprout. When I complain about my wardrobe or my difficult relationships, or when I think moving elsewhere will solve my problems, I'm really demonstrating a lack of trust in what God has deemed good and right. Complaining is telling God we know better than he, that our ways are wiser. But God's Word gives us a different perspective. In Psalm 90:14, we find a prayer that helps us combat our natural bent to discontent: "Satisfy us in the morning with your steadfast love, that we may rejoice and be glad all our days."

So whether we are tempted to think that a different job would make us happier, or a bigger house would solve our space issues, or losing weight would increase our confidence, we can trust that as long as we are seeking the Lord, he promises to give us all we need. We will only find lasting satisfaction in God—his will, his ways, his choices, his timing.

Lord, you are the source of satisfaction in life. Forgive us when we look to the things of this world to meet our needs. Open our eyes to the gifts you bestow upon us. Help us to be satisfied in your steadfast love, that we might rejoice and be glad all our days (Psalm 90:14).

Reflection Questions

1. In what areas of life are you tempted to be discontent?
2. How does your discontent point to a deeper heart issue?
3. How can you fight discontentment in your own life?

17: WHEN FEAR SEIZES YOU

Numbers 13:17–14:4

A couple years ago my husband had the privilege of going to Turkey to speak at a conference for Christian workers. Although I was excited for his opportunity, I was also hesitant because of some terrorist activity in nearby Syria. One practical comfort I had was that we planned to FaceTime every day.

One day during that week, our appointed time to connect went by with no contact from my husband. *Maybe he's just running late*, I reasoned. I looked for text messages… negative. I checked to make sure my ringer was turned up… affirmative. *Maybe he's deep in conversation with someone.*

But as the minutes turned into hours, fear took over. I turned on the news, only to learn that terrorists were active near the Turkish border. Anxiety began to consume me as horrible possibilities started playing out in my head. *Have terrorists overcome the conference and taken captives? What will I do if the worst happens?* My mind went through multiple scenarios: explaining to our children what had happened, looking for a job to support our family, wondering whether to sell the house. By the time my husband was finally able to call I had already decided where to move and how much to sell the house for! Come to find out, he was just fine.

When fear seizes us, all our ability to think rationally evaporates. Life becomes overwhelming and the promises of God seem to fly out the window. When Moses sent spies into Canaan to gather information, and they returned to report to the people what they had found, fear of giants became a more compelling reality than any of the blessings Canaan had to offer, or any of the promises of God to do them good in that land. Although the spies obediently gathered fruit from the land, their report focused on all the seemingly impossible obstacles they faced.

"We came to the land to which you sent us. It flows with milk and honey, and this is its fruit. *However*, the people who dwell in the land are strong, and the cities are fortified and very large. And besides, we saw the descendants of Anak there" (Numbers 13:27–28). As the spies (other than Caleb and Joshua) exaggerated and gave the worst report possible, they compared themselves to grasshoppers and claimed the land would devour them (Numbers 13:32–33).

This fearful exaggeration infected the Israelites, who succumbed to crying and grumbling against Moses and Aaron. It even led them to claim they wish they'd died in the wilderness (Numbers 14:2–3)!

It seems Israel had forgotten God's promise to give them the land of Canaan, regardless of the obstacles that looked so intimidating. "Send men to spy out the land of Canaan, which *I am giving to the people of Israel*" (Numbers 13:2). If the Israelites had truly trusted God's promise, even their enemies in Canaan shouldn't have been a threat to them. God was going to give Israel the Promised Land, just as he'd said to Abraham hundreds of years earlier.

During our moments of fear and panic, God is whispering promises to us too. When anxiety begins to creep in and all the "what-if" situations invade your mind, here are seven things to remember:

1. **God's truth** — *Is what I'm thinking about really happening? Or is it just my imagination running wild?* Paul reminds us to dwell on what is true, honorable, just, pure, lovely, commendable, excellent, praiseworthy (Philippians 4:8).
2. **God's presence** — We can be comforted remembering that we are not alone. God is with us. "God is our refuge and strength, a very present help in trouble" (Psalm 46:1).
3. **God's grace** — God promises to provide us with his all-sufficient grace for every trial that comes our way. Jesus told Paul, "my grace is sufficient for you, for my power is made perfect in weakness." Along with Paul, we can therefore "boast all the more gladly of [our] weaknesses, so that the power of Christ may rest upon [us]" (2 Corinthians 12:9).

4. **God's sovereignty**—God is in control of every situation in our lives. "All the inhabitants of the earth are accounted as nothing, and he does according to his will among the host of heaven and among the inhabitants of the earth; and none can stay his hand or say to him, 'What have you done?'" (Daniel 4:35).

5. **God listens**—Pour out your heart to God in prayer. "I waited patiently for the Lord; he inclined to me and heard my cry" (Psalm 40:1).

6. **God's trustworthiness**—"When I am afraid, I put my trust in you. In God, whose word I praise, in God I trust; I shall not be afraid. What can flesh do to me?" (Psalm 56:3–4).

7. **God's big-picture plan**—No matter how awful this trial may seem, God promises to use everything together for good, for those who are called according to his purpose (Romans 8:28). We may not see the good in our situation at the time, but we can trust God has a hidden smile behind the dark cloud.

So when your child is diagnosed with cancer, or you just learned of a loved one in a car accident, or your husband comes home with news that he was let go from his job, prepare yourself for battle. Don't allow that enemy fear to seize you and take you captive. Fight him off with the promises of God's Word and his unchanging character.

Heavenly Father, when the storms of life surround us, help us to trust your sovereign hand. Remind us of

*the promises of your word so that we can fight our fear
with faith. Give us peace that surpasses understanding,
trusting your goodness and mercy in all things.*

Reflection Questions

1. How does fear feed irrationality?
2. What situations in your life are tempting you to fear?
3. How will you fight fear with truth?

18: THE DANGERS OF DISOBEDIENCE

Numbers 14:20–38

Disobedience has consequences. Raising our four children I often think of the hymn, "Trust and Obey." The refrain says, "Trust and obey, for there's no other way, to be happy in Jesus, than to trust and obey." Our 3-year-old knows these lyrics well, as he's often reminded, "If you disobey then there will be a consequence. We're always happier when we choose to obey."

Sometimes the consequences of disobedience can be painful. A friend tells of a family vacation to Florida. Her daughter wanted to come back home with a perfect bronze tan, but the vacation was only a few days long. Against her mom's clear advice, the girl decided to skip the sunscreen and spent the entire first day on the beach under a cloudless sky. Of course, that's all it took for her to get a sunburn that kept her in agony for days. "I tried to tell her," my friend said to me, "but sometimes you just have to learn the hard way."

During the Israelites' trek through the wilderness, as we've seen, they went through repeated cycles of disobedience, followed by God's anger being stirred and Moses intervening on behalf of the people. Over and over again God was merciful, withholding the punishment they clearly deserved. But when we come to Numbers 14, God has had enough and declares judgment. "But truly, as I live, and as all the earth shall be filled with the glory of the Lord, none of the men who have seen my glory and my signs that I did in Egypt and in the wilderness, and yet have put me to the test these ten times and have not obeyed my voice, shall see the land that I swore to give to their fathers. And none of those who despised me shall see it" (Numbers 14:21-23).

The Lord is angered by the Israelites' constant grumbling against him, along with their refusal to recognize the many miracles he has done for them. Their persistent disobedience and ingratitude have now brought about extremely serious consequences. Among those who left Egypt in the exodus, only Caleb and Joshua will enter the Promised Land; every other person will perish before their wilderness trek has ended.

But God speaks of his "servant Caleb, [who] has a different spirit and has followed me fully, I will bring [him] into the land into which he went, and his descendants shall possess it" (Numbers 14:24). So both Caleb *and* his offspring will be rewarded for his personal obedience to the Lord. In the same way, the judgment upon the Israelites of the exodus will also affect their children. "And your children shall be shepherds in the

wilderness forty years and shall suffer for your faith-
lessness, until the last of your dead bodies lies in the
wilderness" (Numbers 14:33). For each of the forty days
Caleb and Joshua spied out the land, the Israelites and their
children will spend a year wandering in the wilderness.

And so it was. For forty years, the Israelites received
the consequence of their persistent disobedience and
ingratitude to the Lord. If some two million Israelites had
left Egypt, then on average, over the course of 40 years,
about 130 of them died every single day. And every day
their children watched it happen. Our choice to sin not
only hurts us, but inevitably those who are closest to us.
The Israelites' disobedience affected their descendants,
directly and painfully.

God keeps his promises. Near the beginning of their
wilderness journey, when the Israelites were building the
tabernacle, Moses took a census of the people (Exodus
30:11–12; 38:26). In Numbers 26, toward the end of their
journey, a second census was taken. Verses 63-65 tell us
that not one person from the first census appeared in the
second… except for Joshua and Caleb. As God said, all
the grumbling Israelites of the exodus had died in the
wilderness.

This should be a sober reminder to us of the Lord's desire
for complete, heartfelt obedience by his people. Blessings
will come to us when we choose to go his way. But severe
mercies will befall us when we rebel and travel our own
rocky path.

How are you doing in living in joyful obedience to God's commands? Our actions and words reveal the state of our hearts. How we live demonstrates what or who we're putting our hope in, and whether we really believe the promises in his Word. Evaluate your heart today and repent of any stubborn, rebellious ways. And by God's grace, choose to trust that his way will lead to ultimate satisfaction and joy in life. "Trust and obey, for there's no other way, to be happy in Jesus, than to trust and obey."

Father, you are a just and holy God. Keep us from the temptation to go our own way. Help us to walk in the path of obedience, trusting that living by your Word will bring about the most joy in life.

Reflection Questions

1. What do you learn about God's character from this section of Scripture?
2. Are you walking in the path of obedience? Why or why not?

19: PERSEVERE IN GOD'S CALLING

Numbers 27:12–17

Last year my daughter ran on the cross-country team for the first time. Several days a week she practiced for hours, gradually increasing the time and distance she could run. One day toward the end of the summer, she was scheduled to run in a meet on a day of record-high temperatures and blazing sun. As a mom, I was concerned. *Did she drink enough water? Would she have the stamina for the race?* I looked at the course and saw steep hills and valleys — not an easy run. I said a silent prayer for my daughter and watched her intently as the race began.

She started off strong, and in a few minutes had disappeared into the woods behind the school. I waited anxiously as I saw other girls starting to emerge from the woods and climb an extremely steep hill. Finally, I saw the familiar blond curls plodding along. I could tell she was struggling, and everything in my momma-bear heart wanted to rescue her from this grueling race. She tried to run up the steep incline, but slipped and fell. Tears filled my eyes as I saw her determination and heard her coach cheering her on. But she did it. She pressed on against the sun, the heat, and her own exhaustion, finishing her hardest race yet with a respectable time.

Have you ever been in a situation that required much perseverance and determination? I think Moses may have been one of the most determined men ever! Leading a whiny and disobedient people for 40 years, extending grace and mercy to them over and over again, you would think he would have been tempted to quit a hundred times (and at one point he *was* ready to throw in the towel). But despite how difficult his assignment from God was, he persevered to the end.

What's especially fascinating is that he persevered even *after* his chance of entering the Promised Land was taken away. When the Israelites were thirsty and grumbling for water in the wilderness of Zin, God directed Moses to *tell* the rock to yield water for the people. Instead, Moses struck the rock with his staff. Twice. By choosing to disobey and go his own way, he was, in effect, trying to be God to the Israelites. God had a swift and severe consequence for him, "Because you did not believe in me, to uphold me as holy in the eyes of the people of Israel, therefore you shall not bring this assembly into the land that I have given them" (Numbers 20:12). In a matter of minutes, the hope that had been spurring him forward through decades of trials and difficulties vanished forever.

It would have been easy for Moses to be bitter towards God. He had served him faithfully for nearly forty years. And Moses could have objected, trying to claim a right to enter the Promised Land on the basis of what really was a pretty impressive performance. Instead he humbly continued on, leading and serving the Israelites until the last day God gave him. And at the very end of the journey, when they were on the brink of the Promised Land, he pleaded on behalf of his whiny group of followers, "Let the Lord, the God of the spirits of all flesh, appoint a man over the congregation who shall go out before them and come in before them, who shall lead them out and bring them in, that the congregation of the Lord may not be as sheep that have no shepherd" (Numbers 27:16–17).

Even in his weariness and old age, Moses was concerned about his sheep. He knew they needed a leader and pleaded to the Lord on their behalf. The very fact Moses doesn't protest when he's told he can't enter the Promised Land, along with his constant care for the Israelites up to the point of his death, showcases his humility. Moses had indeed persevered to the end.

God typically gives us ample opportunities to demonstrate and learn perseverance. Maybe it's a less-than-ideal job situation, or a difficult relationship that you're ready to give up on. Maybe you feel your marriage is teetering on the brink of disaster. Whatever it may be, James reminds us of God's sanctifying work through our trials, "Count it all joy, my brothers, when you meet trials of various kinds, for you know that the testing of your faith produces steadfastness. And let steadfastness have its full effect, that you may be perfect and complete, lacking in nothing" (James 1:2-4).

Persevering through difficulty is not without purpose. God is completing us and teaching us utter reliance on him.

Father God, help us to persevere in whatever calling you've placed on our lives. Give us grace to keep going, despite obstacles that threaten to overcome us. Let us honor you by persevering to the end, knowing our ultimate reward is yet to come.

Reflection Questions

1. What circumstances in your life have caused you to persevere through difficulty?
2. How does Moses' response to God's discipline encourage your faith?

20: YOU ARE NOT INDISPENSABLE

Numbers 27:18–23

In our family, I've been the primary cook the past 17 years. I enjoy cooking and baking, and have happily served in that role. Over the past few years my oldest daughter has also developed an interest in baking. As I've sought to transfer my limited skills to her, we've enjoyed making cakes and cookies and some dinners together. Already at age fourteen, her skills are surpassing mine.

One Saturday morning I woke up to the smell of delicious homemade cinnamon rolls baking in the oven. Even though the recipe I've always used called for pre-made dough, my daughter had decided to make her dough from scratch. "How did you know how to make these?" I asked in disbelief as I looked at the beautifully spiraled cinnamon bread. "I just found a recipe in your cookbook and followed it." What a sweet reminder that my skills are not indispensable—the very person I was trying to teach and pass them off to was now teaching me.

Moses had done an amazing job leading the Israelites for 40 years. He had persevered through their complaining, interceded for them when God's anger was hot, and led them to the very border of the Promised Land. But due to his failure to obey God in one particular, weighty moment, he would not be allowed to enter Canaan. As we've seen, however, Moses was not angry or bitter. In fact, he demonstrated much compassion when he asked the Lord to appoint his replacement—another man to go before the Israelites as their shepherd (Numbers 27:16-17).

In response, the Lord appointed Joshua, one of only two men from the original group of Israelites who were able to enter Canaan. Moses was to commission Joshua by laying his hand on him before Eleazer the priest and the congregation. He was to transfer some of his authority to Joshua so that all the people would obey him. "And Moses did as the Lord commanded him. He took Joshua and made him stand before Eleazar the priest and the whole congregation, and he laid his hands on him and commissioned him as the Lord directed through Moses" (Numbers 27:22-23).

What a beautiful example of a ministry continuing with a new leader in place. Often times we're tempted to think things will fall apart if we're removed from the equation. We're afraid to give up control and trust that someone else can finish the task just as well, if not better, than we can. I see myself doing this whenever I fail to allow my kids to do certain chores because I think they won't be done well enough. *I'm just going to unload the dishwasher because the kids do it wrong every time. I'd*

better clean the floor myself or it will still be dirty. It can happen at work when we don't ask for help on a big project, exhausting ourselves with long hours because we fear others wouldn't be as thorough. And it can happen in our ministries when we don't invest the time to raise up new leaders because we think there isn't anyone else qualified for the job. *I can't step down from leading Bible studies because there is no one else to do it well!* This kind of thinking stems from pride and can often rob us of needed rest, as well as rob others of opportunities to serve. Pride says, *Everything will fall apart if I'm not involved!* Humility says, *Things could probably start to run even better without me.*

Moses demonstrated amazing humility as, without grumbling or self-pity, he submitted to God's plan for a transfer of leadership. Moses trusted that he was not an indispensable leader.

Joshua, for his part, was deemed "a man in whom is the Spirit" (Numbers 27:18). He was an obedient follower of God, even when everyone around him was rebelling. And now God was rewarding him for his faithfulness. God's purposes will stand despite changes in leadership. Human beings are merely God's chosen vessels to carry out his plans, by the power he supplies.

> *Lord, give us humble hearts that acknowledge our own limitations. Open our eyes to see the gifts of others around us, eager to equip them and allow them opportunities to do your work.*

Reflection Questions

1. In what areas of life are you tempted to think you're indispensable?
2. How can you practically let go of areas you try to control?

21: GOD IS GOD, WE ARE NOT

Numbers 31:1–24

The heartaches of this life are regular reminders that this world is not our home. Even so, when the weight of it all starts to seem unfair we are apt to question if God is truly just, or if he really knows what he is doing. *Why did I have to suffer a miscarriage when my arms long to care for a baby? Why did my friend's 5-year-old child have to get cancer? Why would God allow such a horrific refugee crisis?*

Yet none of today's suffering, be it personal or global, is anything new. The Bible is filled with pain and heartache due to the corrupting onslaught of sin. We see it documented in Scripture in stories of adultery, murder, jealousy, war, floods, betrayal, and ultimately the death of God's own Son. And we see it in how a holy God takes vengeance on sinful people.

Numbers 31 presents the Bible's first example of a truly holy war—a war of extermination. God sent a thousand men from each of the twelve tribes to make war on the Midianites. The ultimate goal was to kill every man, woman, and child of Midian, sparing only female virgins, and launching this war was Moses' final act of obedience before transferring the leadership of the people to Joshua.

In many ways this kind of slaughter can seem like pointless cruelty, but it actually served several vital purposes. Through the war, God was using Israel to wreak his divine vengeance on the Midianite people for corrupting the Israelites (by engaging in sexual immorality with them and persuading them to worship idols). He was dramatically demonstrating to all the surrounding nations God's jealousy for his people. And he was preparing the Israelites for the upcoming wars of extermination in Canaan, the Promised Land.

Our natural reaction to such massive killing might be to question what God is doing. Why does he have to be so severe? Did every one of those Midianites really deserve to die?

What we can so easily forget is that questions like these are based on assumptions that sinful people like you and I have no right to make. We assume that people are naturally innocent and blameless before God. We assume we each have a right to control our own lives. We assume that, simply by being human, we all deserve the love, mercy, and favor of an infinitely holy God, even though we sin against him countless times every day.

We forget that God is not a man, and that man is not God. We forget there is an infinite difference between a righteous and holy God choosing to judge a rebellious people, and the decisions of sinful human beings to exact their own vengeance by killing others made in God's image.

Just as the Egyptians unrighteously murdered the Hebrew babies, the Israelites' killing of the Midianites without an order from God would have been a horrific crime. But God was the one who ordered the extermination. In his unerring hand lies the power of life and death. And his judgment, his justice, is always right.

A similar yet counter example of suffering and blame is described in John 9. The disciples pass by a man who was born blind from birth, and want to know who sinned to cause the blindness, the man or his parents. But Jesus dispels the myth that all suffering is a personal consequence of sinful choices by saying, "It was not that this man sinned, or his parents, but that the works of God might be displayed in him" (John 9:3). Although God does render consequences for sinful choices, suffering is also a means He uses to glorify himself. By healing this man's blindness, Jesus displayed the power and mercy of God to restore sight—a beautiful picture of Christ's ability to make the scales fall off our own eyes that we may see the truth and beauty of the gospel.

When we question God's justice in whatever evil or suffering has happened, we forget what it is we all truly deserve. We are sinners deserving of hell. But by the grace of God and the blood of Jesus Christ, Christians have been forgiven and set free. The question we really need to ask is not, *God, how could you allow this to happen?* but *God, why have I been spared this great evil?* We often forget just how sinful we are.

Almighty God, in your hand is the power of life and death. Help us to trust your wisdom and justice in whatever difficulties arise. Thank you for not giving us what we deserve, but showering us with grace and mercy through Christ.

Reflection Questions

1. What is your reaction to seemingly unjust suffering in your life?
2. How can you cultivate a more God-centered focus when you're tempted to claim your rights and question God's actions?

22: DON'T SETTLE FOR WHAT YOU CAN SEE

Numbers 32

My children have an uncanny ability to hear the crinkle of a candy wrapper from a mile away. As soon as I open a chocolate-chip bag, at least two of them appear beside me in the kitchen. "What are you making, Mom? Can I help?" (This is code for, "Can I have a taste?")

One day when I was making a family favorite that requires unsweetened baker's chocolate, my 8-year-old daughter kept asking for some. Of course, unsweetened chocolate looks appealing, but if you've ever tried it, you know it's like a mouthful of oily, bitter chalk. I tried to encourage her to wait a little while for the finished product—chocolate fudge peppermint ice cream!—but by about the tenth time she begged for a taste of the chocolate bar, I decided it might make for a good lesson.

As soon as she took a bite, her lips puckered involuntarily and a look of disgust spread across her face. "Yuck!" she exclaimed. Lesson learned. My daughter had settled for what she could see right in front of her, instead of waiting for something ten times better—something that required a little patience and trust in mom and her baking abilities. In a similar way, some of the Israelites lacked patience to wait for God's best, and there were bitter consequences as a result.

As the Israelites were camped on the edge of the Promised Land, the tribes of Reuben and Gad, along with half the tribe of Manasseh, seemed to have a change of mind. They noticed that the land of Jazer and Gilead (part of an area called the Transjordan, east of the Promised Land) was rich and fertile, good for grazing their huge herds of livestock. Besides, the tribes of the Transjordan had already been defeated by Israel, and securing the Promised Land was still going to require a lot of fighting.

So these few tribes decided the Transjordan would be a *better* place to settle than Canaan. Even though God had promised *all* Israel a land flowing with milk and honey, and clearly wanted them dwelling in the Promised Land as a single people, these tribes wanted to settle for what they could see. They lacked eyes of faith, and were willing to create a separation between themselves and the rest of the Israelites. They didn't trust that settling in the Promised Land would be more fruitful, and better for all.

Their request to settle in Transjordan wasn't well received. Disunity and discouragement settled over Israel like a dark cloud. Tension mounted as those few tribes made it clear they did not want to go to war: "Don't make us cross the Jordan" (see Numbers 32:5). Moses' anger was rightly kindled as he rebuked them for their selfish desire. "Shall your brothers go to the war while you sit here? Why will you discourage the heart of the people of Israel from going over into the land that the Lord has given them?" (Numbers 32:6-7). Reuben and Gad responded by offering to send their soldiers to help fight for the Promised Land, while the rest of their people settled in peaceful Transjordan (Numbers 32:16-18). Moses trusted their words and granted them their request. In one sense, this was a reasonable compromise. But the stubborn desire of those tribes to seize the first thing that looked good to them—instead of waiting for God's best— eventually had serious consequences.

Once the people of Israel had claimed victory over the Canaanites, the Transjordan tribes celebrated by building an altar. The Israelites in the Promised Land saw this as a forbidden altar and were ready to declare a holy war on their own people. "What is this breach of faith that you have committed against the God of Israel in turning away this day from following the Lord by building yourselves an altar this day in rebellion against the Lord?" (Joshua 22:16). The eastern tribes explained the misunderstanding, but the damage had been done: their insistence on settling outside of the Promised Land had made it impossible for all Israel to live in the kind of unity God had intended for them.

In fact, later in Israel's history, the eastern tribes would be the first to be taken into exile by Assyria for their apostasy against the Lord (see 1 Chronicles 5). How much strife and disunity could have been avoided if every tribe of Israel had trusted that what God had promised would be the best option!

Impatience and unbelief. Living by sight, not faith. Don't we do the same thing? We fail to wait and trust God because we imagine we know better.

I think of women I know who have longed to be married to a Christian man but get tired of waiting and fear being left alone. So they settle for a guy who is passive in his faith, or possibly not even a true follower of Christ. For a while it seems like it will work, but over time his worldly priorities and lack of initiative in spiritual things makes their marriage run aground. Or, instead of trusting God's promises to provide for all our needs, a tight budget causes us to quickly commit to a new job that offers more money — without really praying about our decision or seeking wise counsel. In time that new job drains us of joy and energy, leaving us with little to give to our families.

Waiting for God's best can require us to have eyes of faith. Blessing comes from seeking the Lord's will and trusting he will do for us what he has promised in his Word.

Father, we praise you for your faithfulness! Help us to resist taking matters into our own hands but instead to trust in your promises. Give us eyes of faith and patient hearts to wait for your best.

Reflection Questions

1. In what areas of life are you tempted to settle for less than God's best, as promised in Scripture?

2. How does this passage of Scripture encourage you to not compromise your convictions?

23: TRUST THE PROMISES GOD HAS GIVEN YOU

Numbers 33:50–56, Joshua 7:1–8:2

We're often given promises we don't fully believe or trust. As children we're promised that our parents' rules—limitations on junk food, curfews for teens, and the like—are for our safety and our good. But our rebellious nature tries to convince us that's not really the case. We *want* more fries. We *want* to stay out just one more hour.

God's Word tells us that sex is designed to be delighted in within the context of marriage, exclusively. Yet relatively few people, even among Christians, trust that God knows what he's talking about. *Surely he's being more strict than is really necessary?*

In pursuit of fleeting pleasures, fearing that we might miss out on something better (better than the will of God!) we bypass his promises. But as we disregard the good and the true—biblical promises and their attendant warnings given for our benefit—we start down a path leading only to disappointment, pain, dismay, even disaster. That extra piece of cake today feeds our lack of discipline, tempts others to be similarly irresponsible, leaves us with a stomachache, and over years leads towards obesity and diabetes. A broken curfew weakens trust and invites fresh forms of disobedience. Sex outside of marriage opens the door to a host of issues: guilt, STDs, betrayed trust, broken relationships, and the stirring of emotions intended solely for marriage.

God had promised to give the Israelites the land of Canaan, flowing with milk and honey. But these promises also came with stipulations. So as the warriors of Israel are preparing to enter the land and drive out the Canaanites, God gives Moses one final instruction, a blanket stipulation that applies to every battle Israel will wage within the Promised Land.

> "Speak to the people of Israel and say to them, When you pass over the Jordan into the land of Canaan, then you shall drive out all the inhabitants of the land from before you and destroy all their figured stones and destroy all their metal images and demolish all their high places. And you shall take possession of the land and settle in it, for I have given the land to you to possess it" (Numbers 33:51-53).

The Canaanites worshiped false gods, so God was commanding Israel to make holy war on them. They were to drive out all the people of the land *and* destroy the idols they had been worshiping. God was jealous that the Israelites inhabit a Promised Land swept clean of idolatry.

Indeed, throughout Israel's early history, God repeatedly emphasized that nothing associated with idol worship could be allowed to pollute his people. All these things were "devoted to destruction." If the Israelites did all God commanded to avoid and reject such false worship, promised blessing would follow. But if they disobeyed, God promised trouble.

"But if you do not drive out the inhabitants of the land from before you, then those of them whom you let remain shall be as barbs in your eyes and thorns in your sides, and they shall trouble you in the land where you dwell. And I will do to you as I thought to do to them" (Numbers 33:55-56). Again we see the pattern God sets for us. Obedience results in blessing and disobedience results in consequences.

Following the death of Moses, as Israel's new leader, Joshua, prepared the people for the battle of Jericho, he clarified what things were "devoted to destruction" (Joshua 6:15-19). In effect, this included not just idols and altars, but things of significant material value.

Sadly, one Israelite chose to disobey Joshua's instruction...and all Israel reaped the consequences. Instead of destroying what God said to destroy, Achan stole some of the forbidden things. In response to this grave sin, God made Israel fall before their enemies in humiliation at their next battle, the battle of Ai. "Consecrate yourselves for tomorrow; for thus says the Lord, God of Israel, 'There are devoted things in your midst, O Israel. You cannot stand before your enemies until you take away the devoted things from among you'" (Joshua 7:13).

God's holy anger was unleashed in response to Achan's sin. He was held personally responsible before God and was stoned and burned with fire (Joshua 7:25). Through the death of Achan, God's anger was turned away from Israel. It's a vivid picture of the seriousness of sin and the consequences that can result. Our sin always affects more people than we think it will.

If only Achan had believed God's words and obeyed all his commands, he and all Israel would have defeated Ai in their first battle (Joshua 8:1-2). But in his pride and selfishness, Achan thought he knew better than God. And death was the result.

It's easy to look at Achan's sin with a condemning eye, but are we guilty of the same thing? We doubt God will be faithful to his promises, so we take matters into our own hands, doing what we desire, what we think is best. The temptation of that second piece of dessert is too great to bear, so we give in to the lust of our flesh, forgetting God's promise to provide a way of escape (1 Corinthians 10:13). We let worry rob us of joy and sleep because we don't come to the Lord in prayer and supplication (Philippians 4:6-7). We allow bitterness and unforgiveness to poison a relationship, because we refuse to put on the compassion, kindness, and meekness God calls us to (Colossians 3:12-13).

Every day presents us with countless opportunities to trust the promises of God rather than the faulty reasoning of our own minds and hearts. God is good. His promises can be trusted. And our life will reap much joy, peace, and satisfaction when we choose to take him at his word.

Lord, your way is always right. Forgive us for the times we think we know better than you and disobey your good commands. Help us to walk in the path of obedience, trusting that your ways will bring us the most delight in life.

Reflection Questions

1. In what ways did the Israelites reap consequences for not trusting and obeying God's promises?
2. How have you experienced either blessings for trusting the promises of God, or consequences for choosing to follow your own path?

24: OUR ONE AND ONLY REFUGE

Numbers 35

Where do you flee in times of danger? Our back yard has woods behind it, so we often get various wild animals meandering around our lawn. One warm spring day my daughter, then age 5, was outside playing. I was working in the kitchen while keeping an eye on her from the window. Suddenly I heard her scream and, looking up, saw her running at top speed towards the back door.

"Mom! Mom! Help! There's something from the zoo in our back yard! I think it's a zebra!" Of course, I knew there wasn't a zebra wandering the woods of western Pennsylvania, but as my daughter wrapped her arms around me, I looked out the window and saw a pair of large wild turkeys spreading their feathers. (While we probably needed to work on our animal recognition, in my daughter's defense the turkeys did have some black and white stripes!)

When panic struck, my daughter ran to me for protection and safety. Mommy's arms were a reliable source of comfort and security when she felt threatened by something she didn't understand and couldn't control. I was her place of refuge.

At the end of the book of Numbers, God instructed Moses to create cities in the Promised Land for the Levites, who served as priests. They were to live in 42 cities where they could continue to serve and teach, carrying out their temple duties. They were also to be given six "cities of refuge." These were created as a means of assuring justice for people wrongly accused of murder.

At that time in Israel, the murder of a family member could be avenged at any time by taking the life of the suspected killer. But if such an accused person fled to a city of refuge, he or she could not be harmed until a trial was held. If the death was intentional (murder), the killer would be put to death. If it was accidental (manslaughter), the person was to stay in the city of refuge in peace and safety. When the high priest of that city died, these "manslayers" were free to return home (Numbers 35:28). When their life was in danger, the innocent could flee to safety in cities of refuge.

In several ways these cities of refuge parallel the refuge we have in Christ. Jewish writers tells us that there were roads built to these cities to show the way, and signs stood at major crossroads declaring "Refuge!" In much the same way, we as Christians should be building bridges to show others how to find refuge in Christ. We can befriend our neighbors, coworkers, and relatives who don't know Christ and speak words of truth that can help lead them to the gospel. We can look for ways to meet their needs and open our homes to serve them through hospitality or Bible studies.

Another interesting parallel is that while the cities of refuge were always available to those in need (Joshua 20:4), so Jesus' arms are always open to those who come to him. Matthew 11:28 says, "Come to me, all you who are weary and burdened, and I will give you rest" (NIV). As the accidental manslayer ran to the city of refuge to find rest and safety from the pursuer, so we can run to Jesus to find rest from the trials and burdens of life. In John 6:37 Jesus reminds us that he will never cast out those who come to him. We are safe in his arms.

Finally, just as the cities of refuge provided the only means of escape for an unintentional killer, so Jesus is our only means of salvation from sin. Numbers 35:26-28 reminds us of this truth.

> But if the manslayer shall at any time go beyond the boundaries of his city of refuge to which he fled, and the avenger of blood finds him outside the boundaries of his city of refuge, and the avenger of blood kills the manslayer, he shall not be guilty of blood. For he must remain in his city of refuge until the death of the high priest, but after the death of the high priest the manslayer may return to the land of his possession.

Before the death of the high priest, a vengeful relative still had the right to kill the manslayer if he was found outside the city of refuge. But the death of the high priest served as a sort of atonement for the unintentional death. Only after the high priest's passing could the accused return home free from harm. In a similar way, the death of Jesus is the only true means of escape from suffering the just penalty for our sin. Although many people try to escape hell through good deeds and self-righteousness, Scripture reminds us of our one, true refuge. Jesus says, "I am the way, and the truth, and the life. No one comes to the Father except through me" (John 14:6).

What about you? Where do you seek refuge from the trials of life? Where do you seek peace and forgiveness for the wrongs you have done? Jesus' arms are open to anyone who turns to him in repentance and faith. He promises to wipe our slate clean and give us new life in him. What an amazing gift we've been given through our wonderful Savior!

Thank you, Jesus, that you are our refuge! Thank you for being our safe haven, our shelter. When we have gone down the wrong path in life, may we turn and run into your arms, our sin and shame covered by the blood of the Lamb.

Reflection Questions
1. In what ways do the cities of refuge parallel Jesus Christ being our refuge? In what ways do they differ?
2. Have you sought refuge in Christ? Why or why not?

25: A REASON TO REMEMBER

Deuteronomy 8

Last year, as our family was enjoying some vacation time, my sweet husband was thoughtful enough to download several of our favorite songs we had listened to during our dating years. Some of them I hadn't heard in nearly two decades.

As our family of six piled into the minivan one evening for a drive, Ben hopped into the driver's seat and pushed play on the iPod. Within seconds I was swept up in nostalgia, transported to another time and place—a walk around campus with ice cream dripping down my arm; my husband's first and last football games; the painful heartache of our breakup. Suddenly I was jolted back to reality by a little voice in the back seat, chattering away about what kind of house she'd like to have. One by a lake, apparently. "And I like circle driveways. Do you like circle driveways, Mommy?" My husband smiled at me and suggested, "maybe you should put in your earbuds."

Remembering can cause us to pause from our busy

lives. A song takes us back in time. A picture of an old friend reminds us of laughter and heart-to-heart conversations. The smell of lasagna in the oven transports us to our grandmother's home on Christmas Eve when we were 8.

Memories can also help us see the weaving-together of God's beautiful and perfect plan in our lives. In the middle of a difficult trial it can be hard to recognize what God is doing. But hindsight is often much closer to 20/20, and taking time to remember and reflect on how God has worked in us, even through our challenges, can strengthen our faith in a God who knows the beginning and the end.

When things are going well, however, we often stop remembering, and quickly forget about God. We over-schedule our lives, squeezing him out of our calendars. We get so good at running our own little world that we effectively leave him behind, imagining that we can handle whatever comes along, all by ourselves. This is a place of real danger.

In the book of Deuteronomy, Moses is addressing the Israelites shortly before they enter Canaan under Joshua's leadership. Forty years of wandering in the wilderness has led Israel to this moment, and now Moses is readying them to dwell in the Promised Land faithfully, in fulfillment of God's promise. In chapter 8, he urges them to always remember who brought them there in the first place.

> "Take care lest you forget the Lord your God by not keeping his commandments and his rules and his statutes, which I command you today, lest, when you

have eaten and are full and have built good houses and live in them, and when your herds and flocks multiply and your silver and gold is multiplied and all that you have is multiplied, then your heart be lifted up, and you forget the Lord your God, who brought you out of the land of Egypt, out of the house of slavery." (Deuteronomy 8:11-14)

Full bellies, nice homes, and money in our pockets can be a real temptation to forget about the Lord, so Moses is solemnly reminding the Israelites of God's miraculous deliverance in their lives. Any material blessings they might receive, from food to houses to livestock to money, is all a gift from the Lord. If the Israelites are not careful to keep God's commandments, they are at risk of forgetting him, the very Giver of all their blessings.

The temptation the Israelites are likely to face is that their hearts will be "lifted up," attributing their prosperity to their own power and might (Deuteronomy 8:17). Pride and self-sufficiency puts us on a downward spiral that can lead to all manner of sin and idolatry, with dire, serious consequences. "And if you forget the Lord your God and go after other gods and serve them and worship them, I solemnly warn you today that you shall surely perish" (Deuteronomy 8:19).

God wants to be remembered—for who he is, what he has done, and what he has promised to us—in both the good times and the bad.

During the difficult seasons of our lives, it does our soul good to remember God's faithfulness. There are times of fear, anxiety, and doubt when we're tempted to forget about the Lord and address our problems on our own (which for me often means lying awake in the night, playing out scenarios). Letting our thoughts and feelings run wild leads only to further doubts and despair. But intentionally remembering God's faithfulness to us and to his promises can yield sweet peace and rest.

During Moses' pep talk to the Israelites before they entered the Promised Land, he reminds them to destroy all the other nations in the land, lest they be led astray in serving other gods (Deuteronomy 7:1–4). He seems to anticipate the fear that could likely creep into the Israelites' hearts as they begin to conquer their new land. And Moses addresses that fear, combating it with the sword of remembering the faithfulness of God.

> "If you say in your heart, 'These nations are greater than I. How can I dispossess them?' you shall not be afraid of them but you shall remember what the Lord your God did to Pharaoh and to all Egypt, the great trials that your eyes saw, the signs, the wonders, the mighty hand, and the outstretched arm, by which the Lord your God brought you out. So will the Lord your God do to all the peoples of whom you are afraid" (Deuteronomy 7:17-19).

Remembering ways God has helped and delivered you in the past will give you grace to trust him with tomorrow. Here are a few simple ways to help you in the discipline of remembering.

1. **Keep a journal.** The simple act of regularly writing things down—fears, decisions you're processing through, hopes for the future, remembrances of how God has led you—is a great memory-keeper of God's faithfulness. I love to go back through my journal and see how God has intervened and answered prayer.

2. **Rest.** In our overly scheduled world it takes intentional times of rest to truly be able to think, pray, and reflect on how God has worked in your life. Don't be afraid to schedule some periods of rest into your week.

3. **Share.** God has given each of us a sphere of influence, people in our lives who love us and care about us. Share stories of God's faithfulness with your family, friends, and coworkers. Encourage their faith by sharing your own story.

4. **Pray.** Ask the Holy Spirit to open your eyes to prayers that have been answered and other ways God has been faithful in your life.

5. **Study God's Word.** What better way to see God's faithfulness than through the promises embedded in Scripture? Increase your faith by increasing your time spent in studying the Bible, asking God to help you see his faithfulness throughout time and eternity.

Taking time to reflect on the faithfulness of the Lord—in our childhoods, our marriages, our jobs, our hopes and our dreams—can be a mighty way God strengthens and emboldens our faith. As we remember how God led, provided, and protected in the past, we can trust he will be faithful for tomorrow.

God, you have been faithful in the past and will be faithful in the future. In both the ups and downs of life, give us grace to remember the mighty ways you've worked in our lives. Keep us from forgetting the abundant mercy you've bestowed on us, and increase our faith.

Reflection Questions

1. Why might it be easy to forget God during the good times of life?
2. How can you increase your faith and trust in God through remembering?
3. What is one practical way you'll begin the discipline of remembering today?

CONCLUSION

God is faithful to keep his promises to his people. Just as he promised the Israelites, blessings followed their obedience and consequences followed their disobedience. Due to their stubborn and complaining ways, all of the first generation died during their 40-year journey in the wilderness. But God was gracious to their children and kept the original promise he had made to Abraham to give them the Promised Land.

Throughout the pages of Scripture addressed in this book, we have witnessed the Israelites' constant battle for contentment. When faced with challenges, we have seen them idealize their former life of slavery, grumble against their leaders, and ultimately distrust a faithful and loving God. In all this, we have likely recognized patterns in our own life, when we're tempted to think the grass is greener on the other side or that life would be better if we just had better circumstances.

Yet in the story of these wilderness wanderings we also see Moses, the imperfect but God-fearing leader of the people. From his life we learn about persevering in difficulty, giving grace to those we shepherd, and trusting God's judgments even when life gets hard.

Ultimately, I hope that the greatest thing we've seen in these pages is the vision of an all-powerful, loving, and sovereign God. A God who stretches us beyond what we think we're capable of and sustains us with his never-ending grace. A God who has the authority to destroy kingdoms and create new ones, to cast into hell and deliver from the fire. A God who provides water in the desert, always giving exactly what we need, but not necessarily what we want. This God is the one guiding us on this wilderness journey of life. And we can choose to trust his promises to us, or complain and gripe as we grasp for the comforts we think will make us happy.

As you continue down your own path, remember the ways our great and mighty God delivered the Israelites from oppression. Be mindful of how he has worked in your life, delivered you from evil, and blessed you with more than you deserve. Our wilderness wanderings are not without purpose, but are being used by God to shape us into the people he has called us to be. We can have great confidence that he will bring to completion the work he has begun in us (Philippians 1:6).

Inductive Bible Studies for Women by Keri Folmar

JOY! – A Bible Study
on Philippians
for Women

bit.ly/JoyStudy

GRACE: A Bible
Study on Ephesians
for Women

bit.ly/GraceStudy

FAITH: A Bible
Study on James
for Women

bit.ly/FaithStudy

"It is hard to imagine a better inductive Bible Study tool."
–Diane Schreiner

Keri's studies have been endorsed by...

Kathleen Nielson is author of the *Living Word Bible Studies;* Director of Women's Initiatives, The Gospel Coalition; and wife of Niel, who served as President of Covenant College from 2002 to 2012.

Diane Schreiner – wife of professor, author, and pastor Tom Schreiner, and mother of four grown children – has led women's Bible studies for more than 20 years.

Connie Dever is author of *The Praise Factory* children's ministry curriculum and wife of Pastor Mark Dever, President of 9 Marks Ministries.

Kristie Anyabwile, holds a history degree from NC State University, and is married to Thabiti, currently a church planter in Washington, D.C., and a Council Member for The Gospel Coalition.

Gloria Furman is a pastor's wife in the Middle East and author of *Glimpses of Grace* and *Treasuring Christ When Your Hands Are Full.*

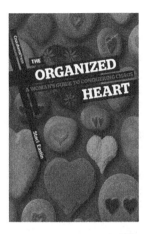

The Organized Heart
A Woman's Guide to Conquering Chaos

by Staci Eastin

98 pages   bit.ly/OHeart

Perfectionism...
Busyness...
Possessions...
Leisure...
Difficult circumstances...

Disorganized?

**You don't need more rules,
the latest technique, or a new gadget.**

**This book will show you a different, better way.
A way grounded in the grace of God.**

"Organizing a home can be an insurmountable challenge for a woman. The Organized Heart makes a unique connection between idols of the heart and the ability to run a well-managed home. This is not a how-to. Eastin looks at sin as the root problem of disorganization. She offers a fresh new approach and one I recommend, especially to those of us who have tried all the other self-help models and failed."
    Aileen Challies, mom of three, and wife of blogger, author, and pastor Tim Challies

"Staci Eastin packs a gracious punch, full of insights about our disorganized hearts and lives, immediately followed by the balm of gospel-shaped hopes. This book is ideal for accountability partners and small groups."
    Carolyn McCulley, blogger, filmmaker, author of* Radical Womanhood *and* Did I Kiss Marriage Goodbye?

Happily Ever After
Finding Grace in the Messes of
Marriage

by John Piper, Francis Chan,
Nancy DeMoss Wolgemuth, and
10 more

**Marriage...Harder than you
expected, better than a faily tale.**

*Published for Desiring God
by Cruciform Press*

PARTIAL TABLE OF CONTENTS

Made in the USA
Monee, IL
21 January 2021